AGENCY ACCOUNT HANDLING

HANDLING

Avoiding Blood, Sweat and Tears

MICHAEL SIMS

John Wiley & Sons, Ltd

Other Wiley Editorial Offices

John Wiley & Sons Inc., 111 River Street, Hoboken, NJ 07030, USA

Jossey-Bass, 989 Market Street, San Francisco, CA 94103-1741, USA

Wiley-VCH Verlag GmbH, Boschstr. 12, D-69469 Weinheim, Germany

John Wiley & Sons Australia Ltd, 33 Park Road, Milton, Queensland 4064, Australia

John Wiley & Sons (Asia) Pte Ltd, 2 Clementi Loop #02-01, Jin Xing Distripark, Singapore 129809

John Wiley & Sons Canada Ltd, 22 Worcester Road, Etobicoke, Ontario, Canada M9W 1L1

Wiley also publishes its books in a variety of electronic formats. Some content that appears
in print may not be available in electronic books.

Library of Congress Cataloging-in-Publication Data

Sims, Michael.
   Agency account handling : avoiding blood sweat and tears / written by
Michael Sims.
         p. cm.
Includes bibliographical references.
   ISBN 0-470-87159-8 (pbk.)
   1. Marketing--Key accounts. 2. Service industries--Marketing. I.
Title.
HF5415.13 .S569 2004
658.8'04--dc22
                                                        2003025316

British Library Cataloguing in Publication Data

A catalogue record for this book is available from the British Library

ISBN 0-470-87159-8

Typeset in 12/16pt Bembo by Laserwords Private Limited, Chennai, India
Printed and bound in Great Britain by TJ International Ltd, Padstow, Cornwall
This book is printed on acid-free paper responsibly manufactured from sustainable forestry
in which at least two trees are planted for each one used for paper production.

To my parents for their lifelong love and support

CONTENTS

PREFACE

*I*n essence, *Agency Account Handling* strives to define the difference between good account handling and great account handling. It has been written for client-facing personnel in all types of marketing agencies, in fact any agency that deals with a creative output. It is a practical handbook that provides guidelines, tips and techniques for those working in agency environments whose remit is to service clients successfully.

The book sprang out of a desire to help agency account handlers and client-facing personnel get to where they want more quickly. Time is too precious not to know the guidelines for excellent client servicing. Account handlers are working with clients day in, day out. If they are wasting time and resources in doing this, they are not realizing their own full potential. If they are not realizing their potential then they are jeopardizing the success of both their career and personal life and the success of the agency. Therefore I have set out guidelines and elaborated on them with strategies, tips and techniques that have stood me and my colleagues in good stead over the years.

It is as much for the new recruit starting out on an agency career as for those account handlers who have been itching for some time to run an account, as well as heads of department who should read this if they want to create environments where people can excel and client business can grow.

This book will help you understand the wider picture of client servicing, give you satisfied customers and allow you to go home at night with a smile on your face. In reality it may not avoid all the 'blood, sweat and tears', but it will certainly reduce them to a manageable level.

You should not expect a list of tricky agency situations with the accompanying 'magic bullet' solutions. This handbook will, however, equip you with the principles and practices to tackle such situations and will leave you in charge of making decisions on the right solutions for your situation. It will allow you to identify the solution more quickly and give you the most appropriate space in which to operate.

My experience has been in direct marketing, brand advertising and digital media, therefore I don't see this book as appealing to only one type of agency sector. It is structured so that account managers wanting to become account directors can realize their dream by focusing not on chasing a job title but on understanding how the step up is made. It is also for graduate recruits who know they will be managing directors one day and want to achieve this quickly (how quickly is up to your personal determination). It is also aimed at agency management (managing directors, client services directors, personnel heads etc.) who want to see the best from their staff and want to create an environment where excellence flourishes. It will help them reduce staff turnover and client attrition and keep their sleepless nights to a minimum.

At college I was inspired by David Ogilvy's books and as a fledgling account handler I was enraptured by some of the personalities and principles of the advertising industry. I would therefore like this book to inspire people to become great at their jobs, pursue their goals and conduct enriched lives. I would also like readers to feel that by doing their jobs successfully they can create enough time and space to pursue their own ideals in and outside work.

HOW TO READ THIS BOOK

This is a handbook for account handlers. It can be read like a novel from start to finish, or it can be used like a Haynes motor manual to fine-tune your performance according to where you are on the road to your success (get used to the clichés, they don't go away).

Each chapter is peppered with specific tips, comments and anecdotes. At the beginning of each there is a list of what you will cover and at the end there is a list of short exercises that will help you analyse your own situation better.

I have included certain sections that will be of more interest to those running client servicing operations – these are in a box with a shaded background.

TIP

Absorbing information from a book can be arduous. I have found one technique particularly useful. Imagine you are reading this book with the aim of imparting it to another audience (e.g. a group of like-minded account handlers desperate for help from you). You are the teacher and you need to digest this material so that you can eventually present it. What you will find is that you will question the content more, use the exercises and consequently retain more. This could be an additional exercise at the end of each chapter (i.e. prepare lecture notes for your own masterclass – eat your heart out, Tom Peters!).

COMMENT

This book should not be read in isolation. What it requires is an openness of attitude, a desire to excel and an agility to juggle a number of activities simultaneously. Hopefully after completing the book, you will challenge yourself to continue your personal development in other areas of your work and personal life.

TIP

The last thing anyone wants to do at the end of a hard day at the agency is to go home and open a book describing the stresses of a working day. Similarly, I wouldn't be seen dead with this type of book en route to my exotic beach holiday. What about negotiating with your boss a 'training' morning at home to get into reading it? And then following that, setting aside half-hour sessions before you go to work? Alternatively, take it to lunch outside the agency. Or leave on time and go to one of those fancy coffee bars and make use of those comfy sofas (foreign language students can't monopolize them all the time).

ACKNOWLEDGEMENTS

I have drawn on a variety of sources for inspiration and have acknowledged my gratitude by quoting them where appropriate. You will also find a complete listing of the reference literature at the back of the book.

I would like to thank Daisy Lilley for approaching John Wiley & Sons on my behalf when I was searching for a publisher. I would like to thank Claire Owen of Stopgap for her support. I would like to thank Sarah Ciccone for the final stages of critical proofreading – it made all the difference.

In addition, I must thank a number of colleagues who took the time to read through my half-formulated first draft and made wise suggestions as to how it could be enhanced. These include Rowan Jackson, Emily Stokes, Janine Yates and Mark Young.

I would also like to thank all those others who encouraged me to start and helped me complete this 'labour of love'.

CHOOSING AN AGENCY

CHAPTER 1

CHOOSING AN AGENCY

In this chapter you will learn about:

- Understanding what you are looking for.
- Working with a recruitment consultant.
- Preparing yourself mentally and physically.
- Getting the most out of an interview.
- How agencies could improve the interviewing process.
- Tips on candidate selection.
- Tips on agency selection.

Both as a candidate and as an employer, recruitment can be a very swift process: pick up the phone to a recruitment consultant, say what you are looking for and let gut feel take over. With this method you may get it right, but you are more than likely to encounter severe problems and get it extremely wrong. While instinct should not be ignored, what this chapter is about is arming the candidate and employer with all they need to go into the recruitment process. Finding a new job or new candidate is a very time-intensive process involving both visible and invisible personal and agency costs. Therefore the risks need to be reduced and the process needs to be as smooth as possible. Much of it is about knowing what you are looking for and optimizing the time at an interview.

PREPARING FOR THE SEARCH AS A CANDIDATE

Whether you are a seasoned player or a raw graduate, you need to take a critical look at yourself before you start your search for your new ideal agency. In essence, you need to know what you are about and what you are looking for.

I will approach this from the aspect of somebody who has already been working in an agency, although the preparation exercises are just as valid for raw recruits.

Something is making you think that a move is a good idea. In order to avoid a premature conversation with a recruitment consultant or prospective employer, take a step back and interview yourself. Ask yourself the following questions.

Why Do You Want to Leave?

Be truthful about the reason. Better job fulfilment, career advancement, nearer location, getting away from your idiot colleague and so on are equally valid reasons and everyone's motivation will be different.

If you are not honest with yourself about your motivation, you may encounter problems. If you are running away from something and you are not facing up to what it is, you may find it at your next employment. For example, a reason such as 'I'm sick of pandering to clients' trivial whims' may uncover a larger issue (let's face it, agencies will always have clients with particular styles). So your suitability for the service industry may have to be questioned.

COMMENT

Often people identify reasons that they feel they cannot share. That was the case with an old friend of mine. He asked my advice, as he knew that ultimately he would be asked this question a number of times by recruitment consultants and prospective employers. Although he did not get on with his boss, that person had an impeccable reputation in the industry and my friend felt that people would think he was the one with the problem.

I understood his dilemma: lack of personal chemistry is a valid reason for moving and I knew people would understand this, but I could see that my friend would feel uncomfortable with such an explanation in an interview situation. This type of discomfort should be avoided, particularly at the beginning of an interview, so I proposed he use a slightly different interpretation of the situation to the recruitment consultants. I suggested he should say that it was the lack of personal development opportunities that was making him move. When it eventually came to telling his current agency, I told him he should say that he had been made an offer he could not refuse.

When he started interviewing, this reinterpretation helped him to be comfortable and focus on the more important matters in the interviews.

What Do You Enjoy/Dislike about Your Job?

Try to deconstruct the elements of your daily routine and grade their importance on a scale of 1–5. Put them in a matrix to see the elements in comparison, like in Figure 1.1.

Element in current job	Score	Desired in next job?
Strategic input	4	YES
Client interaction	3	YES
Internal team interaction	3	YES
Departmental interaction	2	NO
Filing/admin	2	NO
Financial housekeeping	5	YES
Creative product involvement	2	NO
Account business sector	4	NO
Project management	3	YES

Figure 1.1   Current job suitability matrix

What Sort of Person Are You at Work?

You can dissect this in a number of ways, but I would suggest that first you think about what clients and colleagues would say in a *This Is Your Life* situation.

Are you fun to work with? How do you cope with stress? Do you go the 'extra mile'? Do you respond well to constructive criticism? Are you optimistic? Would they miss you on their business?

Make sure that you consider all the angles. Interviews can bring things out of the closet that even surprise those who are saying them.

People also often ask this question in terms of your strengths and weaknesses. Choose a weakness that does not conflict with your suitability for the job or that you can turn into a positive (e.g. 'I used to be incredibly disorganized and not good at time management, but I asked to go on a course and now I enjoy the kick of being efficient with my time').

TIP

Agencies are interested in the three Ps (Passion, Pride and Performance). Group your characteristics into these three categories and provide examples to illustrate them. ('I think the clients will miss me because they have valued the ongoing competitive review that I initiated.')

What Sort of People Do/Don't You Get on With?

This is important inside the agency, but also in relation to the type of clients you can work with. Remember, you may have different likes according to whether it is a work or social context. I think this is something you need to spend time looking at. Think of your friends, colleagues, clients and suppliers. List the reasons you get on with them, can work with them and have a productive relationship with them. In contrast, look at those relationships that do not seem to work.

TIP

Don't confuse effective relationships with friendships. As an ex-client of mine says, 'I have enough friends at home. I don't need to like the agency people as friends, but I do need to respect their work and judgement.'

What Do You Think of Your Current Agency Culture and Style?

If you have not been at another agency, talk to other colleagues who have. They have an automatic comparison in their heads. For your next agency, do you want funky creative, a 9–5 working regime, small and intimate or bigger and networked?

Bear in mind that different styles and sizes of agencies bring different issues. When I moved to my current position, I was looking forward to the intimacy of a small agency after being at an agency of 200 people. Looking back it was definitely the right decision, but it did take me time to get used to the change in size. Even though I had worked in smaller agencies and rationally I knew it would be a radical change, it was the practicalities that made it sink in. With a larger agency comes an infrastructure that is not appropriate for a smaller agency.

So be ready to be flexible: one minute you may be presenting million–pound strategies, the next you may be changing the toner on the laser printer. You need to work out your own preferences based on your experience and what you know you like.

Where Do You Want to Be in Five Years' Time?

I can hear the groans to this question from here. Yeah, your uncle asked you to think about that when you left school but you still don't know the answer. See it in these terms and it may be easier: five years from now, *Campaign* magazine requests an interview with you to create a personal profile. What do you want that profile to say? What steps would you need to take to get there? (For example, if you are going to be a retiring dot-com millionaire, shouldn't you at least take that PowerPoint course and start reading the *Financial Times*?)

What Position Are You Looking For?

Are you looking to move up a level at the same time? Find a less demanding role? Move into a new area? Whatever you want to do, that is fine as long as you can convince both yourself and then others of your desire.

The recruitment consultant will provide the sanity check, but remember to be prepared to be challenged. Some years ago, I interviewed someone for a senior account manager role who was then an account manager. I thought he would be able to make the move up until I asked him why he thought he could handle a position one level above his current position. He became flustered and talked about being very committed and enthusiastic. Until that point I believed he could handle the role. If he had demonstrated a few examples of how he had acted in a senior account manager capacity in his current role, I would have continued in my belief. Yet his response showed me he did not believe in himself at this level.

How Have You Made a Difference in Your Current Job?

Thinking about this will help you understand what you will contribute in the next job. Remember that when you talk about campaigns and client servicing, prospective employers want to know what specifically you did to achieve the objectives.

What Type of Agency Environment Are You Looking For?

You may be able to answer this very easily because of your experience. Otherwise, pretend you are a client and ask yourself what brand (philosophy, approach), people, location, resources (department functions) and accreditations you are looking for. (See Chapter 3 for pointers.)

TIP

Write down the answers to these questions. You may think that by considering them in your head you can shortcut the process. However, you will find that what is in your head and what comes out on paper show different stages of evolution.

In addition, talking to somebody about your answers will also start them make more sense to you.

HOW TO WORK WITH A RECRUITMENT CONSULTANT

Advertising and marketing recruitment consultancy is a crowded industry. You will encounter variety in function, quality and size.

I do not intend to recommend any particular ones, as personal preference and individual relationships are key. If you read the marketing press and talk to colleagues, you will have no problem in identifying and contacting the best consultancies.

Here I am interested in how you work with them, both as a candidate and an employer.

As an Employer

In some agencies' minds, recruitment consultants occupy a plankton-filled environment along with estate agents, lawyers and loan sharks. Others think the opposite and develop strong, very productive relationships with consultants. My view is that the latter group will get better candidates and be involved in a smoother, shorter process.

Whatever your opinion, ignore recruitment consultants at your peril. The danger is that instead of being an ambassador within the marketplace for your agency, they become unhelpful suppliers, provide second-division candidates and/or do not want to work with you. My recommendation is to develop good working relationships with the individuals within the consultancies. Keep them appraised of recent developments, creative/strategic credentials and the senior management team. Also inform them of how you wish to work with them (financial terms plus working procedures – see later in this chapter). A number of the major recruitment consultants are ex-agency, so they can be very helpful in terms of any recruitment processes. Also they are always interested in new credentials (face-to-face recommended) and recent creative work.

To work with a recruitment consultant effectively I suggest the following:

1 A written recruitment brief (see example Figure 1.2).
2 Up-to-date agency information (printed or electronic).
3 Agreement on communication channels.
4 Agreement on financial arrangements (commission/probation period/exit payback).
5 Honesty and spirit of partnership.

Recruitment Brief

We Do Great Work
A G E N C Y

Position Required:	Account Manager
Date:	23rd November 2007
Issuer:	Michael Sims
cc:	Finance Director/Personnel
cc:	ABC Recruitment
	Acme Partners
Process:	Send any candidates' CVs directly to M. Sims. Arrange interview time with Penny Anderson, his PA. Feedback will be given within 24 hours after interview.
Communications:	E-mail (msims@wdgwa.com) or phone (switchboard: 0209 1234567)

Requirement
Account Manager reporting to Account Director, working on pan–European digital media strategy and implementation for Donky Cars.

Client Background
Donky Cars has been We Do Great Work Agency's largest client for three years. Donky Cars is a top five car manufacturer which is now pursuing an 'e-commerce only' sales distribution policy. The agency handles the private and fleet markets for the major European markets and is the exclusive supplier of digital strategy and customer communications for Donky.

Job Purpose
To assist in the client servicing of Donky Cars for WDGWA, delivering digital strategy/campaigns to high satisfaction standards.

Role and Responsibilities
• Assist Account Director in development and implementation of account and major campaigns
• Liaise with central client on campaigns
• Run singlehandedly minor digital campaigns to satisfaction of client
• Maintain account admin (including client correspondence and finances)
• Liaise with other European market clients on translation activity for campaigns
• Coordinate with project management and creative department to deliver client campaigns
• Supervise outside suppliers and partners
• Create and maintain project files and creative guard book
• Manage Account Administrator

Skill Set Required
• Good digital campaign management skills
• Pan-European coordination experience essential
• Languages an asset (preferably French)
• Good admin and project management skills
• Potential to manage team members
• Feels comfortable with sophisticated creative products

Personality Traits/Skills
• Outgoing, confident, flexible
• Good at building relationships (face to face and virtual)
• Good communication skills
• Enjoys challenges
• Enthusiastic, committed and passionate

Personal Experience
• 1–2 years in digital agency or dot-com environment
• Automotive experience an asset
• Consumer and B2B experience ideal

Remuneration
• Salary $xxk
• No car
• Annual agency-wide bonus (after nine months of employment)
• Health cover (after three months)
• Life cover (four times annual salary at employment)
• Company pension scheme (agency will match up to 3% of personal contribution after one year of employment)

Brief approved by

Figure 1.2   Sample recruitment brief

As a Candidate

Ultimately you need to realize that your relationship with the recruitment consultant is influenced by the fact that it is the employer who pays the consultant's commission. The consultant's client is the agency, not the candidate. So the bad news is, in terms of priority, you are not No. 1. The good news is that, as a good candidate, you can make yourself a desired commodity.

Over the years I have worked with a number of consultants as a candidate. You will end up only using a few because of your personal preferences. For this reason, I would suggest that you maintain and nurture these relationships over the years.

In order to get the best out of your relationship with recruitment consultants, I would recommend the following:

1   Decide how many different consultants you wish to work with to ensure good coverage of the marketplace (more than three starts to get confusing).
2   Be prepared for the core questions (see previous section).
3   Develop a good working relationship (they may go the extra mile for you).
4   Agree on the communication channels (also describe your office environment so they understand your particular need for discretion).
5   Make sure you sell both yourself and your aspirations well, as they will need to sell these on to employers.
6   Make a list of the agencies/opportunities that you discuss with a particular consultant (these will then be off limits to the other consultants).
7   Be prepared to talk about what salary package you are on and what you would like (be comfortable with such conversations).
8   Don't accept all suggestions if you are not interested.
9   Identify the better consultants who invest in you as though you will be a future client of theirs.

TIP

There is a lack of professionalism in any recruitment consultant who sends your CV to an employer without your permission. Make sure that their policy is to discuss any opportunities beforehand.

HOW TO PREPARE YOURSELF MENTALLY AND PHYSICALLY FOR THE INTERVIEW

It's funny how some people love job interviews and others see them as the proverbial trip to the dentist's. Whatever the case, you are the one who has initiated the process so this is your spotlight, the time to show your star quality, to move from amateur hour to a full recording contract with fans mobbing you at the stage door. It is a performance you need to rehearse and one that should delight your audience.

There is a whole industry of literature about job interviews. I will only concentrate on the main areas that are particularly relevant to agency recruitment.

Before the Interview

- Find out everything you can about the company through websites, recruitment consultant's brief, yearbooks, cuttings, ex-colleagues.
- Find out what type of work it does and what clients you would be working on and seek out information accordingly.
- Find out the background of your interviewer(s). Try to find any common ex-colleagues etc. (but be careful).
- Confirm time and location and plan your timely arrival accordingly (a sweaty, out-of-breath arrival won't add anything to your performance).
- Be prepared.

COMMENT

Be prepared for anything. When I was an account director, I was sitting as a candidate in the reception area of a potential employer waiting for an interview and was discovered by my senior account manager, who was picking up a friend for a drink.

Friends have had scrapes with tramps, goose droppings (yes, in central London!) and anarchic lifts that have left their attire not of interview standard.

Then potential employers can add their bit to the unpredictability of interviews as well. Forgetfulness, interviewing people for the wrong job and constant interruptions are just the more common occurrences.

TIP

A written-out version of standard questions and answers can be very useful. You should not learn anything off by heart, but it is very good to focus your mind on the tube, bus etc. when you have rushed out of the office with your mind on other things.

- Psych yourself up. Sports psychologists could recommend a whole range of positive thinking activities here. I find a good technique is to play the interview in your head, understanding where the pitfalls (and solutions) and highpoints could be. Then tell yourself you are really going to enjoy it and so is the interviewer. And really believe it.
- Do not schedule any early-morning meetings if you do not function very well at that time.

During the Interview

- The first person you will probably encounter is the receptionist. This is your first opportunity for your star to shine. Do not forget that often interviewers elicit feedback from all those who have met the candidate.
- First impressions are incredibly important, as the first thing in the interviewer's mind is how you will appear to the client on first meeting.

COMMENT

In these days of dress-down Fridays and agency casuals, the choices are difficult. Do you go for the casual look or do you risk appearing stiff? I think ultimately in the majority of cases you have to go for the safe option of a suit or equivalent. However much your Prada open-toed sandals cost, you should remember the first thing on your interviewer's mind, i.e. the initial client impression. If the client is a youth marketer on the web, your micro scooter might work out. I let you make that decision.

- Remember the handshake and eye contact code and make the interviewer feel within 10 seconds that the next hour is not going to be a waste of time – quite the reverse.

- You need to put your stamp on proceedings even before you sit down. Don't be afraid to talk. Break the ice, make that impression.
- You may want to find out about the following in order to decide whether the job is for you:

Agency
- Size of agency (no. of staff, locations)
- Department/functions and resources
- Senior management personnel
- Positioning
- Major competitors
- Major clients (and activity undertaken)
- Partnerships/network affiliations
- Turnover (income vs billing)
- Age
- Culture/management style/spirit of agency
- Working hours

Account
- Structure of team
- Activity undertaken for client
- What clients are like and what they would say about agency
- Prospective boss
- Role and responsibilities
- Potential of account
- Reputation within agency
- Good and bad points
- Predecessor(s) on account and reasons for leaving

General
- Agency social life
- Awards
- Agency attitude to personal development and training
- Potential direction for agency

TIP

Remember to dig deeper than the surface with your questions. For example, if you ask about the creativity of the agency, check the number of awards they have won recently, ask them to show the campaigns they are most proud of and ask what their clients would say about the creative work.

After the Interview

- Be prepared to give feedback on your interview and your interest in the agency to the recruitment consultant (tackle any issues such as something going wrong, because the consultant will get to hear of it).
- If it goes to the next stage, ask to meet the managing director, creative director, the team and someone from a similar level but different account. It will give you a good insight into what working there would be like. (Although you may initiate it, treat each meeting like a further interview.)
- Confirm salary package elements once you get more serious.

HOW AGENCIES COULD IMPROVE THEIR INTERVIEW PROCESS

The reality of the marketplace dictates that there are not enough skilled, experienced account handlers for the number of positions available. Having said that, agencies still have not really caught on to smartening up their act when it comes to the recruitment process. There are still too many stories of missed interviews, job offers without budget sign-off and egotistical interviewing. If you are responsible for interviewing new candidates, you may want to think about the following:

- Make sure that, before you approach the recruitment consultants, you have internal sign-off on the brief and the salary budget from the head of the department and the finance/managing director.
- Take the time to write a recruitment brief. Putting your requirements in a brief will focus your thoughts and deliver better-quality candidates (see example on Figure 1.2).
- Tell each recruitment consultant which other consultants are being used.
- Agree the communication channels (e-mail, phone or post; fax is unfortunately very indiscreet).
- Agree timing of feedback on candidates (maximum 24 hours should be a target).

- Be aware of the sensitivity of the situation. Treat candidates and their CVs as you would your own.
- Maintain discretion and confidentiality throughout the process.

TIP

Your most effective way of recruiting may be through employees within the organization. Make people aware that if they introduce a successful candidate there is a financial reward.

Before the Interview

Everybody seems to know what to do for an interview, but the time never seems to be available to do the basics. Here they are:

- Send directions to agency.
- Book a room in advance with refreshments (try to make it away from your office, and general interruptions).
- Make sure that the room and reception are tidy.
- Have a copy of the brief at hand.
- Have a copy of the candidate's CV at hand.

TIP

1 There are normally a few minutes when the candidates are waiting in reception. What about having an envelope containing the brief (minus salary details) and information on the company for the candidate to read? This scores a few first impression points.
2 What about creating a written matrix of required experience, characteristics and skills that you can use during the interview (see next section and Figure 1.3)?

COMMENT

A friend of mine had three offers on the table. They were all from agencies working in the airline sector. The agencies were large, medium-sized and small. The opportunities were different but all quite appealing. She had real problems in deciding, but set

	Candidate 1	Candidate 2	Candidate 3
Pan-Euro digital experience	3	4	2
Client fit	4	2	3
Agency fit	4	4	3
Languages?	French	French/German	French/Italian
Automotive?	No	No	Yes
Coordination/project management skills	3	3	3
Star quality	4	3	2
Presentation	4	3	3

Figure 1.3 Candidate suitability matrix (out of 5)

everything out in writing to help her decide. In the end, it was the agency culture and style category that decided it for her. She described it as the 'clued-up nature' of the agency, but it was interesting that she repeatedly mentioned the CD-ROM of the agency credentials that they mailed to her house before her first interview. Enclosed was a postcard from her potential boss, which also conveyed a personal touch.

The Interview

There are a number of styles when it comes to interviewing candidates. Whatever your style, you should allow candidates to do most of the talking so you can assess their suitability. Nevertheless, make sure you sell the agency and the opportunity.

I would structure a typical interview as follows:

2 mins	Tea/coffee/settling in
2 mins	Explanation of interview procedure
5 mins	Whistle-stop agency credentials
5 mins	Job function description
10 mins	Candidate talks about experience
10 mins	Candidate talks about reasons for moving/suitability for position
5 mins	Candidate asks question about job/agency
15 mins	Candidate is asked questions
5 mins	Candidate asks any more questions
2 mins	Wrap-up/description of next steps
1 min	Candidate is thanked and shown out

OK, you cannot be that precise, but I aim to allow the candidate to be the one who shows star quality.

COMMENT

I know of one candidate who was not that impressed with an agency but knew the opportunity was very interesting. When it was time to go, instead of thanking him for his time and showing him out, the interviewer asked him to come back for another interview but left him at the door of his office. The office was in the middle of a large work area on the sixth floor and the candidate had no clue where the lifts were. He realized later that this unconscious 'sink or swim' mentality was probably this interviewer's management style, confirming my friend's earlier suspicions, and therefore he refused a second interview.

Here are some suggestions for general interviewing techniques that may help:

DO	prepare (room, brief etc.)
DO	be on time
DO NOT	cancel
DO	stage-manage your environment
DO NOT	allow yourself to be interrupted or distracted
DO	state how you wish to conduct the interview
DO	make sure you have a clock in view
DO NOT	look at your watch to keep time
DO	keep notes (but alert the candidates to this at the start)
DO NOT	ask unacceptable questions or witness this without intervening (see below)
DO	be aware of your own body language (and theirs)
DO	ask open questions
DO	ask candidates to substantiate claims with anecdotes/evidence (e.g. 'Give me an example of how your clients see you as passionate')

COMMENT

Written notes, including a structured matrix as recommended above, have a number of advantages. First, they help you make decisions and they can be given to another interviewer. However, you should agree on the criteria together beforehand.

More importantly, if for any reason a rejected candidate pursues a court case against a prejudiced rejection, there is written evidence that may substantiate that rejection.

TIP

Did someone say *court case*? Let me draw your attention to equal opportunities legislation and the list of sample questions below. The principle behind the legislation is to make sure that questioning and consequent selection are conducted on the basis of relevance to the job concerned. For example, whether you are married or not does not affect how you perform your job.

Unacceptable Questions

Under the Sex Discrimination and Race Relations Acts, it is unlawful to discriminate against job applicants on grounds of sex, marital status or racial origin. Questions asked during interviews may show an intention to discriminate if they reflect assumptions about one particular group or if they are only asked of women or of men or of certain racial groups.

The laws may seem quite complex in their potential interpretation if you are not familiar with them. An example would be to ask women whether they intend to get married or to start a family. This might not be discriminatory in itself if it is a genuine requirement of the job that employees are single and remain childless; however, a good deal of this type of questioning is discriminatory because of the underlying assumptions. For example, the reason for asking this question may be based on the assumption that once she is married or has children, the woman would leave the company because her husband would automatically become the breadwinner.

In essence, it is important that there is a good reason for asking questions, that no discriminatory assumptions are made and that questions pertain solely to the actual fulfilment of the job.

If you are aware that another interviewer is asking an unacceptable question, you need to intervene, or if there is no opportunity until the end, apologize then and reassure the candidate that the answer will not influence any decision making.

Examples of unacceptable questions:

- Are you single or married?
- Are you pregnant or intending to become pregnant?

- Who stays at home when the kids are ill?
- How many days off work did you have last year because of your disability?

I suggest that if you are interviewing regularly, you should familiarize yourself with the Equal Opportunities laws (*http://www.eoc.org.uk*) and read some books on specific interview questioning.

SELECTING A CANDIDATE

First, evaluate your notes and your summary matrix (see Figure 1.3).

One interview will not be enough. You will need to ask your colleagues to interview the best candidates, but I would suggest you give them a similar matrix so that you have a basis of discussion.

For candidates you are really serious about, ask them to prepare and deliver a 10–15-minute presentation on a campaign they have worked on. This should be in front of a panel of colleagues.

MAKING AN OFFER

There are three steps involved in making an offer:

1   Before making an offer, reconfirm with 'the powers that be' that this is still OK.
2   Reconfirm with the candidate or recruitment consultant a) their willingness to accept the offer; b) their notice period/start date (very important); and c) if they have any concerns.
3   Make a verbal offer followed up by a written offer.

SELECTING AN AGENCY

As an outstanding candidate, you will come to the point where you have to decide which one of your numerous offers you will accept. I would suggest another selection matrix (yes, another!) such as the one in Figure 1.4.

	Agency 1	Agency 2	Agency 3
Agency positioning/culture			
Account			
Account team			
Boss			
Opportunity			
Package			
Location			
Fit with personal plan			

Figure 1.4 Agency selection matrix (out of 5)

Whatever you decide, you need to be open and fair with those agencies making offers. Remember, this job may not work out and you could be in the marketplace again very soon.

EXERCISES

1 Use the matrix in Figure 1.1 to evaluate your situation.

2 Which candidate would you assume the interviewer would select based on Figure 1.3?

3 Do you interview people? Ask if there are any training courses or books in your agency. Practise your technique on a colleague.

STARTING TO WORK WITH
A NEW CLIENT TEAM

CHAPTER 2

STARTING TO WORK WITH A NEW CLIENT TEAM

In this chapter you will learn about:

- How the agency can ease the induction process.
- Starting off on the right foot.
- Doing your homework on the client.
- Getting organized.
- How you can help your team and client work with you more effectively.

Your working life is about to take a new turn, whether you are the employer or the newcomer. As an employer you have just hired someone whom you hope will make a difference to the client and the agency. As a newcomer you have just let yourself in for an accelerated change in a number of areas: location, daily travel, working environment, colleagues, working practices etc. This is an exciting time for employer and employee alike.

I used to work in a larger agency where we recruited a number of university graduates each year. The buzz added to the rest of the agency was noticeable. It provided an injection of energy that benefited everyone from the MD to the finance department. Similarly, in a smaller agency, a new addition will change the dynamics of the agency environment. Therefore both employer (MD or team leader) and employee should embrace the excitement.

It is crucial that the newcomer settles in quickly. Both the agency and the newcomer can facilitate this process.

COMMENT

Rowan Jackson, someone whom I admire greatly in the area of change management and operational development, comments: 'You may not be aware of it, especially if the company makes the induction process particularly effective, but you will encounter what is known as the Transition Curve as you go though the first weeks or months of your new job.' The curve looks like the one in Figure 2.1.

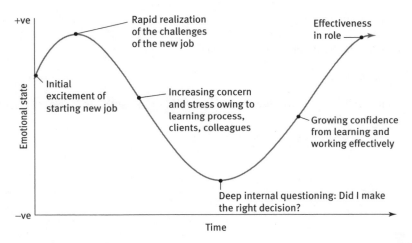

Figure 2.1   Graph of emotional state depending on time in job

The time it takes to go through this curve varies, but can be anything from a couple of weeks to six months. The rate at which you transition through the curve depends on personal and business circumstances.

HOW THE AGENCY CAN EASE THE INDUCTION PROCESS

If you are an employer, take a few minutes to think about your first day at your current agency. And at your previous one? And at the one before that? It was probably a bit like school, when you thought you would never remember which classroom was where. The first week at a new job can be daunting, even for a hardy account handler. Some people think that this 'in at the deep end' approach is character building. It may be for certain people, but it is not productive and it slows down client work.

Quite naturally, friends of the newcomer will ask them how it was in the first week. Imagine that these friends are your most profitable clients. Here are a few guidelines to impress the newcomer's friends:

- Invite the new member to join the team for an informal drink at the agency or a local bar a few days before starting. (At least there will be a few familiar faces on the first day.)
- Set them up with a 'buddy', an account handler who is at the same job level as your new team member, but on a different account. This person can help them understand the day-to-day workings of the agency and offer a different perspective than the account team.
- Before your newcomer begins you may wish to think about:

  - PC set-up.
  - E-mail and telephone arrangements.
  - Business cards.
  - Informing personnel/finance department.

- Get them to come in a little later so that everybody is in place.
- A typical first day could look like:

10am	Arrival
11am	Agency tour
11.15am	Desk/phone/computer/voicemail etc.
12.30pm	Personnel/P45 handover
1pm	Team lunch
2.30pm	Account background by team leader
4pm	Key people introduction

- Structure the newcomer's induction so that they become familiar with other departments, their functions and the client's business.
- Make sure that the newcomer has a suitable introduction to the client. The team leader or immediate supervisor should be there as an endorsement and the newcomer should be given a few minutes to say a few words about themselves.

- Orchestrate a lunch with the MD (maybe with other newcomers) in the first month. This allows a personal connection in the larger agencies and a family atmosphere in the smaller agencies.
- Allow a forum for feedback about the induction process.

If you conduct regular inductions you may want to think about a newcomer's welcome handbook. This could incorporate:

- History and positioning of the agency.
- Ownership structure and sister/partner agencies.
- Structure of departments.
- Clients and what the agency does for them.
- Explanation of core agency process.
- Key personnel.
- General administration.
- Guide to the PC network.
- Guide to the building and the locality.
- Security and fire procedures.
- Local shopping/services.
- Eating out.
- Ordering taxis/couriers.
- Structure of first day/week.

COMMENT

It's tempting to invite new staff to attend meetings on the first day, to get them au fait with client dynamics as soon as possible. However, if you're heading into a heavy meeting with contentious issues, consider leaving them out. It would be a memorable first day if you spent it watching your new account team fighting with a supplier or another department, but it might not leave a great impression of the workplace.

TIP

Chocolates work quite well as a welcome gift as they attract the 'chocoholics' in the agency who strike up a conversation with ulterior 'chocomotives'. Other things such as welcome e-mails, account handling handbooks and so on can be also introduced.

NOT SO UNUSUAL FIRST-DAY HOWLERS

1   Newcomer arrives and new boss has gone on holiday, forgetting about the newcomer's first day.
2   No desk or phone for the new recruit.
3   Business cards printed wrongly.
4   Creative team introduce themselves to the new recruit at a client meeting, thinking that the newcomer is the client.
5   Newcomer, after surviving the first day, walks into the fuse cupboard thinking it is the exit.

STARTING OFF ON THE RIGHT FOOT

As a newcomer you want to create the right first impression. If you are a senior member of the team, the pressure is on to act with confidence and knowledge as soon as you set foot in the door. Luck would have it that joining a new company tends to happen just after you move accommodation, you go on that well-deserved holiday or you are recovering from the long-promised client thank-you bash. So all the good intentions of preparation go out of the window.

But remember, the pressure is on. So you still need to prepare and it can be quite effortless.

Doing Homework on Your New Client(s)

There are some quick, low-involvement devices to allow you to have an informed conversation in your first week:

* First of all, understand exactly what activity is undertaken for which part of the client company and which other agencies work with the client (this should have been gleaned from the interview, but a phone call to your prospective boss will clarify this).
* Confirm which three other companies compete with your new client and what trade magazines you should read.

- Visit the client's website and those of the competitors. Note branding; products being promoted; latest press releases; and interesting market-ing devices.
- Understand the product/service(s) by reading product literature; talking to the enquiry line; and making visits to retail outlets.
- Evaluate the enquiry/ordering system of the client and its competitors by being a mystery shopper.
- Talk to ex-colleagues who have worked on similar products.
- Review the last two months of marketing press and trade press at the local library (about the client, competitors and other agencies).

COMMENT

You do not have to do any of this, but it will increase your confidence on the first day. I was in a meeting with a newcomer to our team. She had taken the time to subscribe to the product and had a pretty good idea how she would improve the enquiry process. I noticed that this sharpened up the other members of the team who had been too concerned with campaign logistics of late. Also she had the luck that when meeting the client for the first time, it was the client who brought up the imperfections of the enquiry centre. This meant that in her first client encounter she created a connection straightaway, and in fact this preparation stood her in good stead for her first proposal.

Your First Few Weeks

After the first week you should make sure you know:

- Your team.
- The client's business.
- Key agency personnel.
- House admin. procedures.
- Building and locality.
- PC/e-mail/voicemail systems.

In your first few weeks you will notice that people are waiting for you to make that first impression and that they listen to your suggestions with surprising freshness (to the chagrin of others). This is a tricky time because while you need to make an impression, nobody wants to hear 'Oh, at the Acme Agency we did it like this. . .' all the time. Also, if you are a senior player you are expected to have a vision, leadership qualities and knowledge that will save the world – all in the first week, and perhaps without having worked in a particular sector before. How do you impress when you have never worked in the complex sector of pipe cleaners and this is where your new client is active?

A few recommendations:

- Make sure you have a rudimentary knowledge of the marketplace (see homework section).
- Discuss with your boss your plan of action (see next points).
- Get the planner, strategist or lead account handler to take you through the marketplace dynamics and consumer perspective. Do this one to one to develop a good relationship. Remember to prepare questions on competitors, key issues, target audience, route to market.
- Get the creative director or dedicated creative team to talk you through the creative work. Prepare questions on objectives, budget, effectiveness, process etc.
- Get the strongest account team member to talk you through account procedures and client personalities. Prepare questions about the effectiveness of campaign mechanics, politics and other agencies.
- Meet the finance director/managing director and ask him/her to take you through the financial history of the account. Prepare questions about income targets, profitability, utilization rates etc.
- Get key personnel on the account together (planner, creative team, account team etc.). Make it a manageable group and get them to talk about the agency, account team, creative work and strategy as if they were the clients. You need to prepare this role reversal so that it doesn't fall flat. Using open questions, the momentum of different subject areas and the informality of a drinks session, you can create a very revealing and productive session. People will tell you more because they are using the clients' voice (you can also have people representing the voice of the agency to get the other side). The participants will also get something out of it themselves. The result is that people feel that you are in control and that you are already contributing.

- For general purposes, identify quickly the key players who can make your life easier:

  - Your boss.
  - The petty cash supervisor.
  - The account planner.
  - The IT manager.
  - The car parking attendant.

- When you finally meet the client, you should have more understanding of the account and the agency. Normally you meet the client at the next scheduled meeting. If possible, do it differently: identify your corresponding client contact, ring up and introduce yourself, and suggest that you go over there to have a one-to-one meeting. The purpose of this meeting would ostensibly be to have an introductory chat and then meet the rest of the team. In reality, you are taking the first step to develop a working relationship and to understand the real client perceptions quickly. In preparation, take a client satisfaction survey (see Chapter 4) or verbally go through the different areas with the client so that you know where you and the agency stand.

TIP

Taking a wild example, if you have not worked in the pipe cleaner sector before and are worried about this, draw up a list of all the possible similarities there could be between pipe cleaner communications and your experience. You can drop them into your first client conversation and see if they have validity or not.

GETTING ORGANIZED

At some point when you want to reach the heady heights of management, you will decide that you have to shape up and become more efficient in your personal organization. You will be reading a book on management and it will state that getting organized in the small and big scheme of things can have a tremendous effect on your success as a manager. You will then start thinking whether you should get a PDA (a personal digital assistant – a palmtop to the majority of people). With this you will join twenty-first-century yuppiedom and think that you have to leave your anarchic fun and creative side behind in the cupboard along with your student 10 pin bowling trophy. Well, first of all, do not lose that anarchic side – it will keep you challenging things. And before you spend a lot of money on that combination PDA/mobile phone/digital camera, let's look at the principles of personal organization. We will look at how you can start cheap and then work up to the latest PDA if you want.

COMMENT

Why wait to become a managing director to get organized? Start now as you move into your first/next agency or after your holiday. The reason for getting organized? It makes you look smart in front of clients and colleagues. It shows that you know what you are doing. It saves you time and money (yours and the client's). It saves your colleagues time and money. It gets you out of the office earlier. It secures confidence in you. It means that your mother gets those flowers on time and you do not miss dates or anniversaries.

Start with the Basics

Get a diary or a good printed calendar and start integrating your work and social appointments into it. When meetings are booked, note them. Use pencil for flexibility. Carry it around with you so that you know when and where you should be. If you want to get fancy, use colour to differentiate the importance of events (e.g. red for a hot date, beige for financial adviser appointments). But make sure you only have one diary – life is complicated enough.

Centralize your addresses, contact numbers etc. in a card index system or a PC address database. This will rid your desk of all those loose business cards and Post-it® notes. If you go electronic, then persuade your team to invest in a business card scanner. It will save time in the long run.

Organize your workspace. Can you find anything that people leave on your desk? Is it an uncharted jungle into which you may decide to travel one day? Here are a few tips:

- Reserve five minutes at the end of the day to tidy up.
- Institute a filing system for your admin. It unclutters your desk (and consequently your mind) and if you are run over by a bus, a freelancer could come in and seamlessly take over.

- Don't let trade magazines that you should read stack up. If they are there after two weeks, file them. Life is too short to feel guilty about good intentions. Otherwise, go on a long train journey and read all that backlog of *Campaign*. On that subject, reading client trade press is essential – don't see it as an extra or a luxury.
- Don't allow 'desk creep'. This happens in two forms: one through your colleagues' mess starting to take over your desk; the other through your boss moving their unfiled correspondence onto your desk. A firm conversation and/or an easy filing system is needed.
- If you have a good filing system for the account team, it stops people wasting your time by asking you location questions ('Hey, where do we keep the cost estimates?') and two minutes of getting up from your desk and looking for a file that the person could have looked for themselves.

Establish time management planning tools. Simply seen, this is a daily 'to do' list with a prioritization of activities. Here you list all the activities, cross them off with a self-satisfied smile when complete or carry them over to the next day. In order to make this work, observe the following rules:

- Give yourself 15 minutes at the beginning of the day to create your to do list.
- Go for the tricky high-priority tasks first. This is worth focusing on. A study of successful managers (into why they were successful) produced the finding that the timely ability to tackle thorny issues was the single most influential element that made them more successful than their contemporaries.
- The grid in Figure 2.2 can show you which activities should be prioritized.
- You may also wish to read Stephen Covey further, as he discusses this sophisticated prioritization in more depth. In his book *The 7 Habits of Highly Effective People* (1989), he maintains that the focus should be on Quadrant II activities (High Importance, non Urgent). This is because they deal with building relationships, long-term planning, prevention and maintenance and these activities are high impact, long term and results oriented.
- Give yourself 15 minutes at the end of the day to see what you have achieved, what you should sort out and what needs to be done tomorrow.

	Urgent	Not urgent
Important	ACTIVITIES: Crises Pressing problems Deadline-driven projects	ACTIVITIES: Prevention, PC activities Relationship building Recognizing new opportunities Planning, recreation
Not important	ACTIVITIES: Interruptions, some calls Some mail, some reports Some meetings Proximate, press matters Popular matters	ACTIVITIES: Trivia, busy work Some mail Some phone calls Time wasters Pleasant activities

Source: Covey, Stephen R. *The 7 Habits of Highly Effective People.*
New York: Simon & Schuster © 1989 Stephen R. Covey. Reprinted
with permission from Franklin Covey Co., www.franklincovey.com.
All rights reserved.

Figure 2.2   Time management matrix

COMMENT

Managing your time is always going to be difficult in a service industry. Yet it is worth doing – not so that you can do more (well, you can), but because it gives you the space to decide whether to do more to secure a worthwhile reward (client satisfaction, internal brownie points, promotion, bonus) or devote more time to personal activities. Whatever you decide on, you will feel good and be seen as smart because you are the one taking control.

20 Top Tips for Managing Your Time

As we are on the subject of time management, here are a few quick tips for your working day that may save time. (Also don't forget the courses and books that specifically cater for this subject.)

1   Make telephone calls in blocks.
2   Prepare notes for telephone calls.
3   Do your thinking in the morning and your doing in the afternoon.
4   Make sure you can see a clock from your desk and in meeting rooms.
5   Create agendas for meetings and circulate these beforehand.
6   Start and leave meetings on time.

7   Create comprehensive action plans after meetings.

8   Evaluate the use of face-to-face meetings vs e-mail and the telephone.

9   Complete one job before you start another.

10   Create your own in/out filing trays.

11   Have a tidy desk.

12   Find a 'quiet' zone for thinking and writing.

13   Don't be afraid to say no.

14   Control and avoid interruptions.

15   Store up questions for colleagues.

16   Encourage colleagues to ask questions in blocks.

17   Use voicemail/e-mail wisely.

18   Have a list of key telephone numbers visible near your phone.

19   Be aware of your own limitations.

20   Avoid time-wasters.

TIP

The Germans have a word, *Erfolgserlebnis*, which means a sense or experience of success. Make sure that each day you experience this on a small or large scale. Before you leave work, think about the things you have achieved during the day (maybe by looking at your action list). It will make you feel more positive and conscious of your contributions to the job (major and minor) and show how you are making a difference.

Also allow colleagues to have access to your diary and suggest that you should have access to theirs. This encourages openness, teamwork, collaboration and ease of arrangements.

COMMENT

So what about that snazzy PDA? Well, get the systems organized first. See how they work and make a choice about the electronic organizer. I would suggest talking to other colleagues and the IT function to discuss compatibility with the organization's e-mail, enterprise systems and your mobile phone.

10 Reasons to Get a PDA

1   The data can be backed up on your PC so that if you lose the PDA you can replace the information.

2   It integrates diary, time management and contact database systems.

3   It helps you work well with colleagues/PAs.

4   Everything is stored in one place.

5   It can be expanded by third-party software.

6   E-mails can be read and written in boring meetings and then sent automatically when back at your PC.

7   It is great for frequent travellers (for reasons of both space and weight).

8   It records expenses as you incur them.

9   It is linkable to other PDAs and mobile phones.

10 The latest editions are great talking points.

HOW YOU CAN HELP YOUR TEAM AND CLIENTS TO WORK WITH YOU BETTER

The principles for working with your team and working with your client are quite similar. Therefore apply the following suggestions to both audiences. (We will return to these principles later on.)

- First, get to know your colleagues and clients as people (use the questionnaire in Figure 2.3 as your guide). You will save a lot of time, even embarrassment, when you can say you know what their preferences are and so on.
- Let people know what your preferences are in the work context. It will reduce the number of wrong expectations.
- Agree your regular communication channels (are we talking faceless e-mails or personalized meetings?). This will depend, but discuss a menu of options.
- Let people know your daily whereabouts and holidays. Give them access to your calendar.
- Change your voicemail each day to incorporate a message saying, for example, that you will not be available in the morning because of out-of-house meetings.
- Set up client guard books to include:

  - account history
  - account structure
  - strategic background

Client Knowledge Questionnaire

We Do Great Work
A G E N C Y

What details do you know about those you work with?

A.
Title_____ First name_____ Surname_____
Normally called_____ Nickname_____
Job title_____ Job function_____
Department_____ Grade (if applicable)_____
Address details_____
Communication means (switchboard, direct line, fax, mobile, e-mail)_____
Home address/phone number_____

B.
Birth date and place_____
Hometown_____
Any things to remember_____
Smoker/non-smoker_____
Diet/alcohol preferences_____

C.
College/university_____
Qualifications_____
Previous companies_____

D.
Outside interests/sports_____
Marital status_____ Partner's name_____
Partner's occupation_____
Children (ages and names)_____
Car_____
Conversational interest_____

E.
How many years working at company?_____ Previous departments_____
How many years working with agency?_____ Main contact_____
What do they use agency for?_____
Other agencies they work with and on what?_____
View of agency_____ Potential client satisfaction_____

F.
Long-range business objective_____
Long-range personal objective_____
Greatest concern at present – business_____
Greatest concern at present – personal_____

Figure 2.3   Client knowledge questionnaire

- campaign history and results
- creative work.

This will save a lot of time on client presentations, new business pitches, client queries and new personnel inductions.

• Decide on the frequency and length of status meetings and stick to them.
• Have informal social events with clients and the team.

NB   Not all answers need to be recorded on Figure 2.3, but you should be aware of the answers to all these questions. If you understand the background to your client and their motivations, you can demonstrate empathy much better and start to understand their thinking.

EXERCISES

1   Review your systems. Where are you wasting your time?
2   Complete the personal knowledge questionnaire for your main client.
3   Think how you can improve your status meetings.

THE DAY-TO-DAY
RELATIONSHIP

CHAPTER 3

THE DAY-TO-DAY RELATIONSHIP

In this chapter you will learn about:

- What clients want.
- Managing the client relationship during campaigns.
- Producing an effective creative briefing.
- Creative presentations to clients.
- Managing problems with a creative concept.
- Moving concepts effectively to campaign execution.
- Effective campaign communication with internal departments and clients.
- Working with the creative product.

*I*n this chapter we will look at the underlying principles of how to service a client effectively. First of all, we need to understand why clients come to agencies and what they expect of them. Then with this in mind, we will look at how teams and partnerships can be built and how they function effectively.

WHAT CLIENTS WANT

If you ask any two contacts from the same client company what they are looking for in an agency, you will get different answers. Similarly, two different companies competing in the same sector may have different requirements. I am sure that initially the global marketing director of IBM would say something different from a managing director of a fledgling dot-com company. Yet when you dig deeper you will find similarities, although each client will prioritize them differently according to their experience, scale, the number of agencies used and their routes to market:

'I want an agency that understands my complex company and is willing to think on my behalf and put my company at the centre of the agency's priorities.'

'I want an agency to demonstrate a good return on marketing investment.'

'I want an agency to be proactive and make me look good.'

'I want an agency to come in on budget and never give me nasty surprises.'

'I want an agency I can trust to deliver.'

'I want the agency always to tell the truth and never be "groveling".'

'I want an agency that has the ability to work with us in the US and in European countries.'

Whoever you ask, you will get two categories of answers. These I call primary criteria and delivery criteria.

Primary criteria are the reasons a client company would be initially attracted to a particular agency, the reasons pitches are initiated and often how agencies are selected. Delivery criteria tend to be the answers that govern an existing relationship. They are how the primary criteria are delivered.

Primary Criteria

Marketplace Knowledge

Client companies with limited resources and relatively little market experience need agencies to guide them in the marketplace.

Sector/Media Experience

For example, in the late 1990s digital media agencies were very much in demand when client companies started recognizing the web and the importance of converging technologies.

Capabilities

You might be the only agency able to handle fulfilment of digital pipe cleaners. Congratulations, you have cornered the market.

Partnerships/Networks

For example, as companies such as American Express and British Airways become more and more global, a worldwide network agency becomes essential. However, another example may be if an agency is working exclusively with a technology third-party partner with which the client company is interested in working.

Vision

Not only do you, as an agency, know where the market is going, but you know where you want the agency to go and which clients you want to work with. Clients admire this smartness, want to be associated with such a company and would like the agency to create that type of action for them.

World-Class People

The people at top of the agency will embody the agency's vision. On a daily basis, clients want to have people working on their business who also have this smartness and who they know will add to their business and their professional lives and ensure quality delivery. Passion, enthusiasm for the client product and energetic idea generation are critical functions of outstanding client–facing personnel.

Creativity

Whether the creativity is in the ideas or tangible creative products, it is both the most important criterion and potentially the biggest red herring if seen in isolation. The creative product is the expression of the agency and is often what clients select at pitch stage. However, remember it needs to be a function of the other primary criteria or it will be toothless.

Delivery Criteria

Speed to Market

Working with agencies is a form of delegation. Not only are client companies looking for expertise they do not have, they are wanting the work done more quickly than if their organization did it in–house. This is worth bearing in mind, as some agencies slow down to the client's pace. Consequently, as clients get frustrated by their own internal departments, they will get frustrated by the agency (more so because the agency is paid to act quickly).

Quality Delivery

This could be regarded as the translation to the creative product (from the interpretation of the client brief by the agency). It could be the accuracy of project management. It could also be in the detail of foreign language translated copy.

What we are talking about here is the client's perception of the agency getting it right first time. This is really the most important delivery factor and we shall return to this again in subsequent chapters. However, it is worth noting that in the client's mind agencies are allowed to make major mistakes as long as errors are corrected fast.

Professionalism

Efficiency, honesty and integrity are admirable qualities in a working relationship. They are worth nurturing, as an account handler needs to use this goodwill in difficult times.

Personal Relationship

Clients value a strong personal relationship with agency personnel because they see the benefits of this. A good relationship can enrich their business and personal lives. They can call in favours when necessary. Agency personnel can also be very loyal and will go the extra mile for their clients.

Cost Efficiency

Overall value for money could be meant here, but it is also the cost efficiencies achieved through the buying power skills and market knowledge of the agencies.

COMMENT

Another way of seeing what clients want is how an ex-client of mine sees what she needs from an agency:

- **Ability** – the ability to deliver the results necessary on time and to satisfaction.
- **Relationship** – something built around a partnership where the agency almost acts as an outsourced marketing department. This means knowledge of business, individuals, preferred ways of working etc.
- **Trust** – bound together with honesty, no lies or bluffing and a desire to meet and exceed expectations.
- **Integrity** – sealed with a mutual respect and a professional understanding of each party's areas of expertise.

It is now worth thinking about your own situation. What does your client want from your agency and what priority do they set on the individual criteria?

$$\text{VALUE FOR MONEY} = \frac{\left(\begin{array}{c}\text{Agency Product} \\ \text{+ Client Results}\end{array}\right) + \left(\begin{array}{c}\text{Agency Delivery/} \\ \text{Quality of Service}\end{array}\right)}{\left(\begin{array}{c}\text{Cost of Staff} \\ \text{+ Production}\end{array}\right) + \left(\begin{array}{c}\text{Emotional Cost of Doing} \\ \text{Business with Agency}\end{array}\right)}$$

Figure 3.1   Client perception of value for money

It is a complex combination that is difficult to deconstruct (we will look at how to do this in Chapter 4 when we talk about client satisfaction). However, it could be expressed by a client as 'value for money'. Look at the equation in Figure 3.1.

There are a number of points worth discussing here:

- 90% of clients will use results as their overriding criteria in the value for money equation.
- There is a perception among clients that agency staff do not appreciate the importance of the financial aspects of campaigns. Sure, they understand cost estimates, but they don't grasp the crucial nature of the budget. It is not their money and they are not as respectful about budget limits, campaign effectiveness and return on investment. Personally I think this criticism is partly valid. Seasoned account handlers do get it, but others less so. This does not imply that they are irresponsible with the client's money. It is more the fact that, as the budget is an unintegrated account of the campaign, it is paid less respect. There are occasions when the client does not provide a budget but asks the agency to come up with ballpark figures on how much it should cost. Such an approach is understandable and gives the agency flexibility, but it does not strengthen an agency's relationship to and its discipline with the budget. Campaigns where an allowable marketing spend per unit is established initially are examples of more accountable, 'integrated' campaigns.
- Some account handlers concentrate on the delivery criteria only to strengthen the relationship. This is necessary and can lead to greater profitability. However, don't forget the primary criteria; they need to be maintained to keep major competitive advantages in the marketplace.

- Seek to understand the emotional cost of doing business with the agency and do not underestimate it. This is where delivery criteria do need to be focused on. Two examples will illustrate the emotional cost:

  - **Example 1.** Client A needs to deliver a seminar at a trade show. In the past she has worked with Agency X and Agency Z. Previous seminars using the two agencies have produced the same format and the same success for roughly the same amount of budget. However, working with Agency X is, as she says, 'like watching paint dry'. Who will get the next seminar business?

  - **Example 2.** Client B loves working with Agency L, but it does not have a good reputation in his department. A tricky new product campaign is being awarded and Client B's tough boss has advised him to use Agency M. Which agency will Client B select?

The rest of the chapter will look at establishing and maintaining a high standard for the delivery criteria. It will be of particular interest to account handlers who are involved in the executional elements.

MANAGING THE CLIENT RELATIONSHIP DURING CAMPAIGNS

If you asked me to say what good servicing is about, I would say it is about *creating, managing and exceeding expectations*. Effective campaign execution works within such a framework.

There will be an initial step where the client initiates the campaign in a meeting/phone call. Particular attention should be paid by the agency to:

- The campaign objectives/results the client seeks.
- Target audience.
- Product/message/media.
- Metrics.
- Timing/time schedules.
- Budget.
- The way the client wants to work with the agency.

The effectiveness of the campaign will greatly depend on the agency's understanding of the above. Make sure they are fully explored with the client.

The next step is for the agency to interpret the client's intentions in a communications or creative brief. This is where the process of the agency 'getting it right first time' starts. A better-quality brief will be ensured if:

- The client has written a campaign brief to begin with. The act of putting things in writing focuses the mind and creates a better overview. If there is a written brief, there will be a more logical briefing and there will be fewer omissions.
- Anyone in the client organization who will have to approve the creative work sees/signs off the brief to the agency.
- The above-mentioned areas are explored verbally in a meeting by the account handler plus other strategic experts (planning, creative director, business consultant etc.).
- Somebody writes a contact report, a record of the meeting to detail the salient points.

COMMENT

Those junior account handlers just starting out can look forward to their fair share of contact reports. Each agency has a different format, but every contact report will include location, date and attendees of meeting plus discussion and action points. I personally find the terms 'agency' and 'client' used in the contact report counterproductive (in fact, emphasizing the usual 'them and us' boundaries) when actual names could be used. For example: 'Client to provide approved URL to agency by March 14.' To me this reinforces the confrontational client/agency battlelines and is not person specific. What about 'Joe Soap to provide Mike Sims with URL by March 14'?

TIP

I find contact reports and status reports a very important necessary evil in running an account. The format and the wide circulation lists scream *dull* and senior recipients leave them in their inbox without reading them. For me, where possible, a letter to a specific contact and copied to other contacts, combined with user-friendly phraseology, is a better way of communicating.

- Any missing information is supplied to the agency before the next stage is undertaken.
- Inside the agency, an inspiring communications proposition is discussed and people are happy with it.
- The client buys into the proposition. Most creative briefs are full of complex information and quite dense to digest. Therefore strip out the two most important parts of the brief: the single-minded proposition and the support evidence. Put these into landscape PowerPoint format (24 point typeface) to discuss.
- The client signs off the expanded brief.
- The creative team and any other interested parties are briefed personally and thoroughly. A creative brief should be involving and in the briefing session everyone should be inspired to go away and produce excellent work. Maybe the location with a relevant expert is the inspiration. Teams can be briefed in art galleries, swimming pools, planes – whatever captures the imagination and does not blow the budget.
- The first review of creative concepts is conducted properly. Time should be allowed for a review and potentially any feedback to be incorporated. At this point the agency team should work as a cohesive unit and come to agreed solutions.

PRODUCING AN EFFECTIVE CREATIVE BRIEFING

Whether you are looking at the actual written form or the process by which a creative team is briefed, the briefing should follow a number of parameters. It should involve, give direction, excite and inspire. This is the stage where the agency picks up the baton from the client brief and initiates or continues a process that can ultimately lead to outstanding work.

It is worth noting that if the client brief has not been formulated to involve, give direction, excite and inspire, there could be a need for a good deal of preparatory work and discussions with the client. Consequently, it is invaluable to encourage the client to create a watertight brief before work begins in the agency.

All briefs should demonstrate:

- Understanding of the brand.
- Clarity.
- Focus.
- Surprise.

Understanding of the Brand

The starting point is the need to understand where the communications fit in relation to and as an expression of the brand. Questions that should already have been answered are:

- What do we want the brand to stand for?
- What does it currently stand for in the minds of our consumers?
- How is our brand different from its competitors?
- How does our brand talk to people?

In formulating the brief you then need to ensure that everything is consistent with the brand and use this communications opportunity to leverage the power of the brand.

Clarity

Vagueness in a brief breeds misunderstanding. If lack of clarity is present both in the client and agency creative brief, it will cause lack of clarity in the creative product. Looking at the following may help you achieve clarity:

- Rethink, requestion.
- Use plain English and avoid jargon.
- Think carefully before using marketing speak – people have different definitions for the same term.
- Think about how you would explain the brief to someone at the coffee machine.

- Check for contradictions.
- A briefing Q&A session will help avoid misunderstanding.

Focus

With over 1300 commercial messages fighting daily for people's attention, being single-minded is key. Moreover, people find it hard enough to take in one point from a piece of communication, let alone two.

Yet we often end up trying to deliver two-pronged propositions! Here are suggestions on how to avoid this:

- Agree on one simple communications objective and one message.
- Describe exactly what you want the customer to do as a result of the communication.
- Weed out extraneous information: are all the facts 100% relevant?
- Avoid cutting and pasting from previous briefs.

Surprise

Consumers have heard your sales pitch before. In reality, people aren't enthralled by the 99th claim this year that your credit card has no annual fee. To make consumers notice, you must come at it from a new angle. This requires an element of surprise.

Achieving surprise could come from:

- Imagining if your product/service were not available. Deprivation research looks at this very factor. (Imagine if they took your car away, how would you feel about yourself, how would you travel to visit friends/relatives etc.?)
- Turning what you want to communicate upside down or reversing it (e.g. Volvo changed from one portrayal of safety to another and showed that a really safe car can allow people to do extraordinary, dangerous things).
- Imagining what a child of six would think.
- Identifying what everyone else in the marketplace is doing and doing something different (the zigzag strategy).

Key Elements of a Written Brief

- The role and competitive context of the communications.
- Target audience/customer insight.
- Customer proposition and accompanying relevant support evidence.
- Call to action and intended measurement of encouraged behaviour.

Questions to Ask about the Proposition

- Is it single-minded?
- Is it surprising, thought-provoking, relevant and motivating?
- Would you understand it if you saw it on a poster?
- Can you defend it convincingly?
- Why should someone be convinced by this rather than by something else?
- Could you explain it to a friend?
- Could you write a headline from it (even a bad one)?

TIPS

1 At the beginning of the creative review, remember to remind people of what the brief was about.
2 Put the single-minded proposition and support evidence on a piece of paper and stick it up on the wall.
3 View the concepts with an open mind. Allow the impact to sink in.
4 Look again at the brief and get somebody to be a member of the target audience – get them to express what they feel about the concepts.
5 When feeding back, be positive and honest, don't direct (articulate the problem, not the solution). Be clear about what you like, not just what you don't like.
6 Agree what is to be presented and when it is to be ready.

CREATIVE PRESENTATIONS TO CLIENTS

I have presented creative concepts in hotel bedrooms, to audiences of 200 people and on a houseboat. I heard once about a client getting pitching agencies to present in a rowing boat in Regent's Park. Everybody has their war stories and no two sets of circumstances are the same, but bear in mind that you can maximize the chances of creating a winning presentation by following some very simple guidelines. They adhere to the simple principles of any presentation: preparation, clarity of purpose and message, connection with the audience and controlling the environment.

1   Be happy that the concepts meet the brief and confident that they will enrapture the client.

2   Creative ideas do not sell themselves. Take the time to rehearse the presentation in front of a colleague and get them to play devil's advocate, coming up with all the tricky questions. Some people will say that this is a luxury, but by doing this you will potentially save yourself a lot of time. In addition, if there is a good deal of down time (travelling in train/car, waiting for client etc.), make real use of it.

3   Ideally, set the meeting on your home turf. Psychologically this will be more advantageous for you: you are on familiar territory and you can stage-manage your environment to your taste. Alternatively, if it is impossible to be in the agency, make sure you are aware of the meeting room (layout, facilities etc.) and arrive early to set up.

4   Assess the importance of the meeting and your capability to present winning concepts (do you need help from colleagues?). Understand it from your point of view and then mentally go around the other side of the table and assess it from the client's perspective:

–   What are they expecting?
–   Who are they expecting?
–   How high is their confidence in you, the agency and the creative product?
–   What is the client's relationship with the creative director/team and other people in the agency?
–   How important is the campaign?
–   Are there any other pressures?
–   What is the quality of finish expected of the presentation materials?

5   You should then decide which members of your team should be there, evaluating suitability, willingness and cost.

6   Decide what will be said, when and by whom.

7   When you have arrived at the meeting, make sure all the props are in place, the projector/video is functioning and there is enough space to move around.

8   Assess the client's emotional state. Have they just been in a stressful previous meeting? Are they looking forward to this meeting?

9   Break the ice with introductions/small talk and teas and coffees so that the atmosphere is not clinical but receptive.

10   Tell the client what stages you are going to go through. Make sure they are happy with this and confirm the timing.

11   The stages could be:

-   Recap on the brief/setting the scene.
-   Reminder of creative proposition/customer insight.
-   Creative approach/idea.
-   Concept presentation.
-   Summing up (checklist of what the concept achieves).
-   Fielding questions.
-   Next steps.

TIP

Your best approach will be to have at the meeting the creative person/team who worked on the brief. Most clients are attracted to the creative spirit. A business-savvy or very good presenter from the creative team, tackling the presentation and the question, can be very successful. However, remember the personal chemistry aspect as well: a number of creative people enjoy certain aspects of client presentations and not others. You will need to decide the mix.

COMMENT

If the relationship between client and agency is good, the client will be looking forward to the presentation. However, it is a bit like one of those home decoration TV programmes where householders return to their property after the briefed interior designer has done a makeover. There is visible tension and nervousness and it can go a number of ways. But remember, they are the ones who will end up having to live in the house. Similarly, the client will have to live with the concept and sell it on further within their organization. Also it is communication about their company, therefore it needs to say the right things about the company they work for. Most importantly, they will be judged inside the company by their evaluation of the concept.

So there will definitely be tension or trepidation, but you can channel it to add to the excitement of the presentation.

12   If you know that the client will have issues with something in the presentation, this is something you will need to resolve. I would bring it into the conversation before showing the concepts and when talking about the creative issues. If the client becomes sensitive about a point, you can say: 'And you will see how we have resolved this when we present the concepts.'

13   You will need to create excitement about the concepts (this could also be done on the phone before the meeting) so that there is an atmosphere of anticipation. But do not oversell.

14   Make sure that you stage-manage your props and that each client contact can see the materials. Don't focus only on the key decision maker, as this will rile the others. People also don't always want to be the nodding dog in the spotlight. However, maintain good eye contact and have the confidence to go through the different stages by telling a story, one that is compelling and it is obvious you passionately believe in.

15   Before presenting, deconstruct what you have to present. Learn it and explore it. Demonstrate your own understanding, passion and belief in what you are presenting.

16   Give your clients the space and time to get used to ideas, concepts etc. If the concepts are tangible, let them touch and feel them.

17   Walk through any clarifications, logistics/costs (be prepared, even if you know you do not have all the answers) and issues. Don't leave anything hanging.

18   Make sure that you leave them with materials/information with which they can sell the concepts inside their organization. At a basic level, these could be photocopies/replicas. Alternatively and more comprehensively, you could put together a pack with a question and answer section and a reminder of the background and brief.

TIP

Whatever creative work is being presented, a written creative rationale can be great to leave behind. This could include:

- What is the purpose of the communication?
- What did we identify as the most powerful thing that could achieve this?
- What was the springboard for the creative idea?
- What is the definition of the creative idea?
- Which executional elements will bring this idea to life?

MANAGING PROBLEMS WITH A CREATIVE CONCEPT

You will often get a situation where a client will not buy a concept. The reason has to lie in one of four areas: the concept itself, the selling of the concept, the receipt of the concept by the client and the client themselves.

You can influence the selling and receipt of the concept along the way by involving the client in the process (at creative briefing), talking through the creative approaches blind (i.e. in advance of the meeting without seeing them) and presenting alternative concepts that help them understand how you have come up with the recommended approach.

Often the problem lies outside the concept and more in the relationship between client and agency and the corresponding management of expectations. I would therefore recommend focusing on preparation before a problem arises. You will have more chance of getting a successful result than of reversing a fait accompli.

So there are times when the agency has come up with a brilliant concept and it is not welcomed because it is too bold, badly timed etc. Unfortunately there is no magic bullet for this situation, but you may wish to act in the following way:

1   Assess the degree of immovability:

  – Check whether the client has understood the concept.
  – Probe the issues and see whether they can be resolved by minor changes.

- Seek to understand whether this is the last port of call (or if the concept can be presented to boss or another member of the client team).
- Use sensitivity so that you don't isolate the client from the concept if it is to be presented to others.

2 Make the client feel they are being listened to.
3 If they remain immovable, get the client to articulate (preferably also in writing afterwards) what the issues are.
4 Discuss what is on the client's mind and talk in the abstract about alternative approaches.
5 Rebrief the creative team (or an alternative team).

COMMENT

This is one of the major stress points in account handling. Remember what was said previously: a client can forgive the perception of an agency not getting it right the first time as long the problem is quickly rectified.

First, the account handler needs to rise above the personal stress. (If you did everything possible, don't waste time blaming yourself; if you didn't do everything, learn and move on.) You need to assess the timing and cost implications and manage expectations accordingly (i.e. alert the client that certain deadlines are in jeopardy, but only after a course of action has been put in place to show the client that the agency is bouncing back). You also need to inspire parties within the agency, particularly the creative team, to rise above the situation and create a new solution. This is possible with practical feedback about the concepts.

Agencies sometimes have problems with learning and moving on. Ultimately, this makes for a 'them and us' situation. Once the teamwork dynamic is lost between the agency and the client or within the agency, it is only a matter of time before you hit a downward spiral. In a manufacturing industry, you would call this hiccup in the process 'rework'. Rework causes time, money and frustration. Ideally, it would be better to get it right first time around. Involvement of the planner or a designated 'strategic planner' on the account (maybe the group account director) is essential. This can expand the creative horizons, focus on a true customer insight and a single-minded proposition and therefore reduce the need for rework. This person, who has a position removed from the client front line and can think from the customer's point of view, should be able to identify issues before they reach the concept stage.

MOVING CONCEPTS EFFECTIVELY TO CAMPAIGN EXECUTION

Running creative campaigns effectively requires:

- A good project management team.
- Good project organization.
- Effective communication.
- Resources/time/money management.
- A clear process.
- Clarity of roles.

Project Management Team

How the executional team is structured really depends on the nature of the campaign and the media being used. Nevertheless, each team member needs to understand what role they play and how they interact with the other team members, outside suppliers, in-house suppliers and the client. Everyone at whatever involvement level needs a sense of ownership. They must feel responsible for the success of the project, be committed to the client and the rest of the team and make things happen.

COMMENT

Effective team interaction is key. A friend of mine is a creative services director and was asked by the managing director to identify what was the problem with a series of projects going through the agency. He sat down with the account director and identified that in addition to a misunderstanding between the creative services manager and the account handler about role responsibility, there was no commitment to achieving the deadline and no respect in the team for one another's expertise. Both account handler and creative services manager were replaced. The new team agreed the roles and the creative services manager was given the project management lead, which created dual ownership of commitment to the client. Things improved greatly.

Ideally, it is better for existing team members to learn from mistakes, as teams consequently become stronger. I am not a fan of agencies merely substituting team members to short-circuit the process. However, in the above case, the situation had become unrecoverable.

Project Organization

Just as you need to be personally organized to use your skills best, a project needs to be structured to use resources efficiently. Project administration revolves around internal and external communications, timings and costs.

Project administration can be categorized and recorded in electronic or hard files in such sections as:

- Client correspondence.
- Market background.
- Creative briefing.
- Internal departments.
- Supplier/partner communications.
- Cost estimates (client).
- Cost estimates (supplier/partner).
- Creative development.
- Production development.
- Legal issues.
- Invoicing.
- Final product.
- Complaints log.

This kind of organization will help things move more quickly and allow clients and other external parties to audit the efficiency of a campaign.

COMMENT

Project management is vastly improved by examining whether all team members know and agree to buy into the overall process. This means that the process is mapped out and adhered to. Has this happened in your agency?

EFFECTIVE CAMPAIGN COMMUNICATION WITH INTERNAL DEPARTMENTS AND CLIENTS

The best communication relationships are founded on mutual trust and confidence in each other's abilities and areas of expertise. When running projects, good relationships can help you achieve personal commitment, the potential of getting something extra, peace of mind and ultimately the desired project outcome.

Time needs to be invested in understanding the personalities and what motivates them. Build personal relationships and try to develop the commonalities. Attempt to understand what pressures they are under, how they will react in a particular situation and what 'hot buttons' they respond to.

A good deal of time and stress can be spared by facilitating the communications process in the following way:

1   Exchange e-mail addresses, mobile numbers and direct lines (and home numbers for emergencies).
2   Know where your contact sits in the office so you can understand the context.
3   Get them to visit your office environment.
4   Agree which communications should be handled by e-mail, telephone or face to face, and which parties need to be included. (NB   Key stages should be done face to face.)
5   At busy campaign times, make sure that everybody is abreast of everybody's daily whereabouts. Also, when timing schedules are discussed, identify any key conflicting dates (e.g. meetings, holidays).
6   Meetings should include:

   –   Statement of objectives.
   –   No distractions.
   –   The right people at the right time.
   –   Summing up.
   –   Agreement of next actions/allocation of tasks.

7   Seek to resolve problems together.
8   Offer thanks and appreciation when due.
9   Be clear, fair and sensitive in any criticism.

10   Instill an understanding of the financial issues related to the campaign.

11   State in advance what is required in terms of financial management/records.

12   Stipulate how and when any amendments to estimates should be communicated (e.g. verbally, then in writing within 24 hours).

13   When a campaign is moving quickly, you need to be flexible. However, always judge new scale and cost/time implications.

14   Try to have major discussions about costs face to face. Take the emotion out of discussions.

15   As you move from step to step, make it clear to partners/team members what the next actions and responsibilities are.

TIP

I am always amazed how seldom people are given thanks for their work. Good clients understand the value of saying thank-you. Once our team received a cake with the campaign icon on it as a token of our client's gratitude. Similarly, when you work with suppliers or colleagues, make sure you encourage them with your thanks.

WORKING WITH THE CREATIVE PRODUCT

If you want to achieve a strong, inspired creative product with good client buy-in and efficient execution, you may wish to consider the following guidelines for the smooth running of the creative product.

1   The creative brief is the yardstick against which concepts and finished creative work should be judged. Make sure that you agree with every word in the brief, particularly the single-minded proposition and the support.

2   Have parties within the organization approve the brief if they will be judging the creative product.

3   Make sure that the creative team and the creative head(s) fully understand the product. Let them see it in action. Let them be inspired.

4   Define what the client should be expecting at each stage (through the project plan).

5   Make sure that everyone is aware of who is involved in the approval process.

6   If you have concerns, question the creative product/concepts for workability (e.g. banner ads, direct mail formats), legibility (e.g. posters), the strength of call to action etc., share these with other colleagues for their views.

7   If photographs or illustrations are being used, make sure that enough examples of previous work are submitted to ensure the desired effect can be achieved. Also don't forget usage fees and their implications.

8   Request paper samples for print materials in advance of production.

9   Remember to request advance printed or electronic samples for internal campaign communications.

The above is the rational route to improving the creative product. Remember that you have to factor in that you are working with colleagues who have a different mental make-up to you. If creative teams were like account handlers, they would be writing contact reports and/or be in your job. Therefore you need to treat them accordingly.

When dealing with copywriters, art directors, designers etc., bear in mind the following:

- Remember that you are closer to the project by virtue of the fact you have attended client briefings, written the brief etc. Think how you can accelerate their learning.
- Teams do not tend to read reams of briefs until the copy development stage. Then they think about, for example, how they can bring appendices to life.
- Teams respect somebody who knows their stuff – don't read a brief out verbatim.
- Remember that the creative team is closer to a concept than you – they are proprietorial and have lived with it longer, so allow yourself time to return with comments when you have engaged with it. (Don't be too dismissive too quickly, but tell them you want to think about it and will come back in an hour/next day etc.) And as previously discussed, use a positive approach to give feedback.
- Creative teams respond to enthusiasm about their product.
- Creativity is linked with a person's sense of worth. Therefore be sensitive to this and approach any criticism from the eyes of the consumer rather than personal taste.

- In order to get under the skin of a creative team, try one day to write some copy and have someone else represent your work to a further person. Then you will know the daily frustration that a creative team experiences. Imagine what can be used to prevent this frustration.
- Thank and reward creatives as you would other team members.
- Allow them to take pride in their work.
- Keep them informed at all stages.

The best relationships that I have forged with creative teams have been those where the following have applied:

- The creative team and I have personal empathy.
- The creative team has a personal interest in working on the account.
- There is creative involvement at the product briefing stage.
- The work requires sophisticated concept development and implementation.
- The creative team has a sense of business reality.
- The creative team has direct access to the client.
- The client has a direct relationship with the creative team.
- The creative work is admired in the agency.
- The creative process is enjoyable for all parties (i.e. we had a laugh working together).

COMMENT

When a team (client/agency and/or account handling/creative) is working well together, it is a true partnership and the sparks that fly from the combination can create inspiration, great work and fulfilment. It is definitely worth aspiring to, because when it clicks, you remember why you got into this crazy business.

EXERCISES

1 Define the priorities of the primary and delivery criteria for your clients.

2 Create a personal profile for the creative team you most liked working with.

3 Detail the personal highs and lows of a) a recent briefing session; and b) a recent client creative presentation.

CLIENT SATISFACTION

CHAPTER 4

CLIENT SATISFACTION

In this chapter you will learn about:

- The value of focusing on customer satisfaction.
- Conducting an informal customer orientation check.
- Instituting a satisfaction review process.
- Improving satisfaction through performance.

Sometimes agencies get so involved in project management or taken up with the end result of the creative product and the associated revenues that they disregard their client satisfaction. All the hard work by the project team is undermined by the fact that the client does not see the value for money or views the emotional cost of achieving a campaign as too high.

For a service organization, an agency can become very inwardly focused, losing its understanding of how to service a client effectively. In this chapter we discuss the importance of maintaining a high degree of client satisfaction and how it can be monitored.

THE VALUE OF FOCUSING ON CLIENT SATISFACTION

If you think of yourself as a consumer, you will know the fickle nature of your relationships (even longstanding ones) with banks, retail outlets etc. Banks are the oft-quoted example where satisfaction is actually low but inertia allows them to keep you and write to you as their valued customer. It is therefore understandable why the relatively new kids on the financial block, such as the telephone and internet banks, captured the interest of the disenchanted.

Nevertheless, there are few of these black-and-white examples. Long-established retailer Marks & Spencer has recently been experiencing difficulties. Ten years ago it was frequently held up as a great retail chain operator satisfying its customers. This example helps us understand that although there is a very strong link between the two concepts of client satisfaction and client loyalty, it is not as obvious as one might think.

I believe it was one of the IT companies which identified that, in the purchase of office equipment, only the very satisfied customers are loyal. If you measure loyalty by a simple question about repurchase intention, then you find out that you have to be very satisfied with the product or service to repurchase. If you look at Figure 4.1 you will see that of the satisfied customers (i.e. those with a customer satisfaction index, or CSI, of 80%), only 16% responded positively to the question about intended repurchase. In contrast,

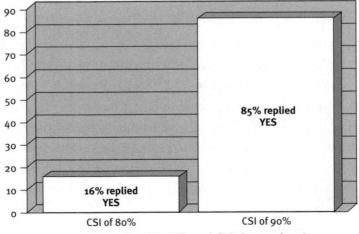

Figure 4.1   Satisfaction/loyalty paradigm

if you have very satisfied customers (i.e. those with a CSI of 90%+), 85% of those customers will reply that they will repurchase the product or service.

The point is that you need to strive for very satisfied customers. Your business depends on it.

Very loyal customers will allow you to promote repurchase very easily and you will find that consequently that promotion is more profitable.

COMMENT

Those who have been in business development and client servicing will grasp this instinctively. At the top end of the satisfaction scale, you can sell something very easily. However, if you take the time to analyse your client satisfaction scores, you may look differently at how you interpret them.

For example, which statement would allow you to gain a better insight and future focus into the following data (percentage of customers rating their degree of satisfaction)?

Outstanding 10%   Excellent 82%   Good 6%   Fair 2%   Poor 0%

Statement A: 92% of our customers rated us as outstanding or excellent.
Statement B: Only 10% of our customers rated us as outstanding.

My answer would be B. Overall the data shows satisfaction, but you need to increase the outstanding quota in order to secure loyal customers and a healthier business. Loyalty really only happens at the outstanding end.

As you reflect on this data, ask yourself four questions:

1   What is the company's present CSI?
2   How can I improve it?
3   What does my management team think about it and what actions are being taken by the team to improve it?
4   How can I improve the data-collection process? (World-class companies collect data from a number of different sources and systematically analyse it.)

CUSTOMER ORIENTATION

Before you start rushing to measure your client satisfaction formally, take a minute to understand what your clients would say to their colleagues

Customer Focus Assessment (page 1)

We Do Great Work
A G E N C Y

	HIGH	MEDIUM	LOW

1 Do you go further for your customers?
- Our clients go away with a smile on their face
- We do not just exceed expectations, we totally surpass them
- We do not have difficult clients, just interesting challenges
- We make sure clients get what they want, not what our systems are designed to deliver
- When our clients talk about our staff, they say 'they go out of our way to be helpful'
- Our staff notice when something needs doing and just do it

2 Do you handle complaints, problems, tricky situations well?
- If in doubt, we believe the client
- Our compensation, when we get it wrong, is more than the client expects
- We always apologize, even if we do not think it is our fault
- Compensation is based on the team member's judgment, not arbitrary rules
- We demonstrate to our clients that we trust them
- The agency demonstrates to the staff that they are trusted

3 Are you proud of the agency output?
- Our output is unique and enthralling
- Our output features compelling principles of design or strategy
- Clients enthuse about our output
- Clients tell other agencies about our output
- Clients feel strong emotional connection to our product

4 Do you get close to your clients?
- We give our clients the small company feel
- We welcome our clients like old friends
- We communicate with our clients as individuals
- Our client-facing staff are great conversationalists
- We use systems to maximize the information provided to our client-facing staff to build a relationship
- Our staff are genuinely interested in our clients and build common ground
- Our staff genuinely like our clients
- The agency treats the staff as individuals
- We make an effort to get know our clients
- The agency recruits for and encourages staff to be enthusiastic about our output and the interest of our clients
- Our clients trust our staff's judgment

Continued overleaf

Figure 4.2   Customer focus assessment

Customer Focus Assessment (page 2)

We Do Great Work
A G E N C Y

	HIGH	MEDIUM	LOW
5 Is your technical wizardry attractive to your clients?			
• Our technical products get our clients excited	◯	◯	◯
• We provide clients with technical products that they did not know they wanted but make them go wow	◯	◯	◯
• Our technical products are cool	◯	◯	◯
6 Do you treat your clients and staff as stakeholders in partnerships?			
• Our staff are 'stakeholders' in the agency	◯	◯	◯
• We ask clients what they want us to do and how they want us to do it	◯	◯	◯
• We put our clients in control of their interactions within the company	◯	◯	◯
• We give regular customers extra benefits	◯	◯	◯
• When clients make comments, we always respond in a suitable time	◯	◯	◯
• When client comments require action, we always act or let them know why we are not acting	◯	◯	◯
• All our clients regularly meet senior management as well as the frontline team	◯	◯	◯
7 Do you have a good general reputation with your clients?			
• Clients think of our products, staff or company with affection	◯	◯	◯
• We have a compelling positioning	◯	◯	◯
• Our corporate image is one that our clients relate to naturally	◯	◯	◯
• We are associated with popular issues and causes	◯	◯	◯
• Our client-facing staff are the sort of people you would enjoy a long train journey with	◯	◯	◯
• We make use of any areas where the company is an underdog to win client affection	◯	◯	◯
8 Do you surprise and delight your clients?			
• We give our clients pleasant surprises	◯	◯	◯
• We make regular surprise changes to our pricing/products	◯	◯	◯
• We surprise our clients with unexpected gifts	◯	◯	◯
• We surprise our lost clients with incentives to bring them back	◯	◯	◯
• We use creative techniques to enhance our originality	◯	◯	◯
• We do things differently from our competitors – so differently it surprises	◯	◯	◯
• We have fun and make dealing with us fun	◯	◯	◯
9 Do you communicate effectively with your clients?			
• We keep up a regular, frequent (non-project-oriented) dialogue with all our clients	◯	◯	◯
• We listen to what our clients say and we act – every time	◯	◯	◯
• We communicate in the way our clients want to be communicated with	◯	◯	◯
• We tell our clients what is happening throughout every transaction	◯	◯	◯

Continued overleaf

Figure 4.2   (*continued*)

Customer Focus Assessment (page 3)

We Do Great Work
AGENCY

	HIGH	MEDIUM	LOW
9 Do you communicate effectively with your clients? (continued)			
• We do not have physical barriers to communication			
• Our website gives clients something more than it does our prospects			
• Our e-mail addresses, telephone numbers, fax numbers etc. are all easy and accessible			
• We have a good voicemail/e-mail system			
• We have real conversations with our clients			
• We aim communication at our regular client contacts but hope to influence the CEO as well			
10 Do you promote your USP?			
• Everyone in the company knows what our USP is			
• We make sure all our customers and potential customers are well aware of our USP			
• We make use of the special capabilities of each member of staff to extend our capabilities			

Source: Brian Clegg, *Capturing Customers' Hearts*, reproduced by permission of Pearson Education Limited.

Figure 4.2 (*continued*)

about you and the agency. Think about how customer focused your operational structure is. Is it tailored to different clients' needs or is it 'one size fits all'?

Brian Clegg identifies that 'An outstanding customer relationship is the only safe way of building differentiation.' Have a look at an adaptation of his client focus assessment from his book *Capturing Customers' Hearts* (2000) in Figure 4.2 and see how you rate. Score how far you agree with each of the statements.

TIP

Use this informal benchmarking survey as a way of getting your team to understand how well the agency works with its staff to service clients. Let them complete the survey, have a discussion session to explore the results, and then identify the areas and the accompanying measures to redress certain client satisfaction issues.

INSTITUTING A SATISFACTION REVIEW PROCESS

If you recognize that monitoring your clients is important, you need to decide how to create your own measurements; analyse and discuss the feedback; and take action.

There are a number of formal and informal ways to benchmark client satisfaction. We will discuss in brief a number of methods.

Client Focus Group

This is where a number of clients are invited to attend a discussion group that concentrates on their opinions about the agency. This is a qualitative method of gathering data about how the agency's product, people and procedures are perceived. Bear in mind the following:

1 It should take place at a neutral venue, somewhere where the clients feel comfortable and can be entertained with lunch or dinner afterwards as a thank-you for their time. Private clubs have been used successfully by various agencies.

2 The person running the group should appear neutral and consequently will be able to elicit both positive and negative criticism. It could be a research expert or someone with the right group facilitation skills from a sister company. The person is there to encourage discussion and be qualified to bring members of the audience into and out of the conversation.

3 The discussion guide should be agreed by senior management and include those responsible for attending to clients.

4 No one from the agency should attend the focus group, but should come later to attend the lunch/dinner.

5 The facilitator should determine the number of attendees, but 10–12 is probably sufficient for one session.

6 The mix of attendees is important: not more than two clients from one company and there should be a broad mix of client companies using the different agency services.

7 Attendees should be invited by the lead account person and what is intended and expected at the meeting should be mentioned in advance.

8   Guarantees of confidentiality, 'off the record' comments and non-specific criticisms should be made at the beginning of the meeting.

9   Feedback to the clients should be given after the meeting once the data has been collated and any specific action determined. The lead account handler should discuss this with the client.

10   The session is not an informal chat but follows a tight qualitative and quantitative process. The discussion process centres on expectations and how clients perceive the agency is performing against those expectations.

Client Satisfaction Survey

Whereas a client focus group may happen once a year, an agency may elect to conduct a client satisfaction survey every six months or after a major project. It is designed once again to measure attitudes about the agency's product, people and procedures. And in fact the client focus group data, captured by spreadsheets, coded, sorted and analysed, can be used to design the survey. (Never create a survey from internal agency points of view – it should be customer focused.)

The survey can be mailed or, ideally, conducted face to face with the client by a neutral party. It should be used on a regular basis as a benchmark for improvement.

COMMENT

Particularly if your business is project based, your project management procedures should include a project satisfaction review.

A satisfaction survey designed like the one in Figure 4.3 should allow you to understand what is important to a client and to do a gap analysis on how the agency is performing.

Lead Account Team Communication

This is an informal way of judging the temperature of the client relationship and satisfaction with the agency. It can be in the form of telephone calls, drinks/lunches or meetings.

Sample Client Satisfaction Survey

Please score the answers to these statements according to the following scale and elaborate on your answers where possible:

The answers to the (a) questions can be scored 1–5 (1=Very unimportant, 2=Unimportant, 3=Indifferent, 4=Important, 5=Very Important, n/a=I cannot evaluate this)
The answers to the (b) questions can be scored 5–1 (5=Excellent, 4=Good, 3=Average, 2=Needs improving, 1= Unacceptable, n/a=I cannot evaluate this)

1
a) I believe that marketplace knowledge plays a ⬭ role in an agency's dealings with our company

b) I would evaluate Acme Agency's marketplace knowledge as ⬭

c) How could Acme Agency improve? _____

2
a) I believe that an agency providing a broad range of services to a client is ⬭

b) I evaluate Acme Agency providing a broad range of services to our company as ⬭

c) Acme Agency could improve by providing the following services: _____

3
a) I believe that the agency being part of a network is ⬭

b) I evaluate Acme Agency providing value by being part of a network as ⬭

c) Acme Agency could provide better value through its network by:_____

4
a) I believe that agencies having excellent senior management personnel is ⬭

b) I evaluate Acme Agency's senior management personnel as ⬭

c) Acme Agency could improve its senior management personnel by:_____

5
a) I believe agencies providing excellent creative work is ⬭

b) I evaluate Acme Agency's creative work as ⬭

6
a) I believe agencies providing strategic input is ⬭

b) I evaluate Acme Agency's strategic input as ⬭

7
a) I believe agencies providing excellent delivery is ⬭

b) I evaluate Acme Agency's delivery as ⬭

8
a) I believe agencies providing value for money is ⬭

b) I evaluate Acme Agency's value for money as ⬭

9
a) The overall service that Acme Agency offers is ⬭

Continued overleaf

Figure 4.3   Sample client satisfaction survey

Sample Client Satisfaction Survey (page 2)

10
Please rate the following functions out of 5 (5=excellent, 4=good, 3=average, 2=needs improvement, 1=unacceptable, n/a=I cannot evaluate this)

	Results	Service	Fees	Ease of doing business
Account Handling				
Planning				
Traffic/creative services				
Production				
Creative				
Finance				
Admin/client communications				
Senior management				

How can improvements be made?_____

11
Any other comments?
_____

Figure 4.3   *(continued)*

Agency Hotline

This is more of a concept than a reality. However, clients should feel that they can channel praise to or ring alarm bells with the managing director. The latter should make it clear by providing mobile/direct line numbers and e-mail address that the client is very welcome to do this.

Status Meeting Checks

Regular dialogue is no substitute for client satisfaction assessment. Some account teams I know build in a 'How are we doing?' five minutes as part of their regular status meetings.

COMMENT

The most important point here is that if you ask 'How are we doing?' (whether formally through a satisfaction process or informally through discussion), you need to show that you have listened and have a plan to remedy the situation. A client friend of mine said he gets at least four satisfaction surveys a year from different parts of an international agency network he works with. Yet each time none of the areas of dissatisfaction is redressed and this increases his frustration.

IMPROVING SATISFACTION THROUGH PERFORMANCE

Once you have identified the areas in need of improvement, you can set about redressing the problems. The principle is pretty straightforward, but take care in deciding what the solutions are.

I suggest that you communicate to the client the fact that you have been listening to their comments and you have devised a number of actions to rectify the situation. Here you should also add a few 'quick wins', including ones you know will appeal instantly. A great deal of hidden hard work may also have to be put into rectifying the situation. You could make this visible so the client can see what is being done. For example, if the client is not happy with the print quality of a regular supply of brochures, detail the additional quality control checks; e-mail the client as each stage is checked; and invite them to selected approval stages.

If you feel that client satisfaction could still be improved and the client has not articulated any particular area, have a look at the following areas to see if improvements could be made in order to become more customer focused:

- Tailoring of agency product.
- 'Can do' attitude of agency staff.
- Belief and trust in client's judgement.
- Compensation and apologies when mistakes are made.
- Sufficient information to do job properly.
- Pride in agency output.
- Client's emotional connection to product.
- Knowledge of client's personal and business circumstances.
- Client/agency partnership attitude.
- Agency positioning/corporate image.
- Attitude and skills of client-facing personnel.
- Empathy with client.
- 'Surprise and delight' methods.
- Client communications.

By asking yourself and your team the client focus assessment questions in the last section, you should be able to come up with ideas to improve the agency's client-facing performance.

EXERCISES

1 List all your client satisfaction monitoring methods. How can you improve on these?

2 How customer oriented are you? Complete the assessment questions for your agency.

3 Write down what clients would say about you personally.

MASTERING THE MOMENT

CHAPTER 5

MASTERING THE MOMENT

In this chapter you will learn about:

- Managing difficult situations.
- Exploiting excellent situations.
- Improving your presentations.
- Getting involved in pitches.

Some time ago I fulfilled a lifetime ambition at the famed Coney Island amusement park: I batted in the baseball practice cages. The stuff of Hollywood movies, this is where a machine fires baseballs at you so you can practise your baseball swing. What I experienced at the beginning, even when I had the machine switched to 'slow' mode, was a torrent of balls hurtling towards me. It was only after I 'got my eye in' that I started to enjoy myself. I began to see them as individual balls instead of a constant barrage and then I turned up the setting to medium speed. Eventually (a few dollars later), I felt as though the ball pitching had so slowed down that I knew when and where to hit it. It felt really sweet and I understood what sports psychologists refer to as being 'in the zone'.

This 'mastering the moment' chapter deals with this very idea. As an account handler, there are a number of balls being chucked at you. You need to decide whether to catch, fend off or make a play for them. Whatever you choose, emotionally and psychologically you need to slow them down, either to evaluate and act or to enjoy the moment.

MANAGING DIFFICULT SITUATIONS

We work in a very stressful business. We have ridiculous deadlines, work with some people who are very good at getting what they want, with other people who have problems expressing themselves, and ultimately we are judged on how we work with all these factors to achieve delivery. Yet we make our work more stressful by being our own worst enemies.

First, we need to admit to ourselves that this is the business we are in. These are not extraordinary circumstances; this is the norm. As marketers, we are by definition problem solvers. By working in agencies, we are being paid to come up with solutions to problems at all points of campaign development and execution. Certain clients use agencies specifically for getting things done more quickly and without the internal hassle. Therefore it is the agency that absorbs that hassle.

There are always going to be problems. In fact, we are destined to make mistakes. However, it is how we solve these problems, handle the hassle and minimize the mistakes that makes us bad, good or great account handlers.

Do you recognize any of these situations?

- Your client rings to give you a deadline for a campaign start that is earlier than the previously tight deadline.
- You need to ring your client to tell them that the brochures have been delivered to Walsall rather than to a trade show in Warsaw.
- The client wants to change the wording of the headline and you need to get the creative team to agree to it.
- Your supplier has let you down but is saying that it was due to a wrong instruction from you.
- Your MD comes to you and wants you to drop everything to work on a pitch that is being presented tomorrow morning.

- You have an important date with your partner and you have to cancel because of a client/agency commitment.
- All the above are happening at the same time.

There is no 'magic bullet' for any of the situations. Yet if you understand the following principles, you may be able to manoeuvre the situation into the zone where you can control it.

So in your sphere of influence are:

- Yourself.
- Information/depth of knowledge.
- Timing.
- The communications climate.
- The message.

These elements will give you the power to control the situation. That power provides you with options; the ability to evaluate and make a decision; and the best way to communicate a message to achieve your objectives.

Yourself

To believe that you can make a difference in any situation, you have to give yourself the best breaks. You need to equip yourself with the mental armour to conquer any problem that should arise. Let's take the initial alarm bells. You receive a call alerting you to the fact that a consignment of brochures has ended up in the West Midlands rather than Central Eastern Europe. There are a number of options:

1   You put the phone down and bawl out your junior.
2   There is no junior so you rush to lock yourself in the toilets.
3   You get on to your clients and blurt out the news.

I suggest that you do not do any of these things. Whatever you do, you need to understand that with this type of bad news you go through an emotional process with the acronym name of SARAH (Shock/Surprise, Anger, Resignation,

Acceptance, Help). With the example of the supplier ringing you up to say that it was because of bad instructions: first of all you can't believe it (surprise), you get frustrated at the thought that such a conclusion could be drawn (anger), you reluctantly give in to the fact it might be true (resignation). Finally, having acknowledged it may be true (acceptance), you look for assistance to solve the situation (help).

Everyone goes through SARAH on receiving bad news. How long the process lasts and how long you get stuck in a phase, such as anger, depend on a number of factors. These are the perceived severity of the situation, your experience, your emotional state and how it is communicated. So SARAH is not a problem, your success depends on how you deal with the situation and how prepared you are for it. We will tackle personal health in a later chapter, but your emotional armour needs to be maintained.

It is interesting and very sad to hear people who have had mental breakdowns relating what actually symbolized the start of the breakdown. While normally it is small things that make people snap, in reality it is the build-up of stress that is the problem. You are not likely to have a breakdown about a very stressful phone call, but what I am talking about is perspective. Many stressful situations in agencies are not viewed from the right angle. Stress, lack of sleep, a heavy workload and so on encourage you to see things out of perspective. Make sure you channel the stress away from yourself regularly, so that when you do have to deal with a potentially stressful situation you can take a balanced view. This balance allows you to make better decisions and glean more information.

For example, your brochure supplier rings about the Warsaw shipment at 6pm on Friday night. A stressed person would have problems listening to the full conversation and want to put the phone down as soon as possible. A less stressed person would try to assess all the facts and start thinking about potential solutions. Someone with a clear head could realize that with a problem occurring on Friday night you probably need people to be contacted over the weekend. You therefore need to make sure you have their mobile or home numbers.

TIP

If you are a person who gets easily stressed, to the point that it prevents you from functioning properly, you might want to explore a few methods to help you out when you are feeling the pressure. (These will be explored more in the personal health section.)

- If the stressful situation is a phone call, ask the caller to repeat the circumstances and take notes.
- Ask if you can call them back, compose yourself and continue.
- Before you do anything, take a number of deep breaths, stand up and walk around.
- Visualize the difficult situation as a Loony Toons cartoon to see the funny side of it.
- Visualize the client congratulating you on sorting out this tricky situation. Then work back to how you arrived at the solution from the announcement of the situation.
- Use a decision matrix (such as Figure 1.4 in Chapter 1) to help you work out your problem.
- Talk it through with someone. (Much of the time the solution is in your head, you just need to hear it expressed.)

You can also develop and maintain your evaluation and decision–making skills to be ready to face challenges along the way.

Agencies are full of horror stories about crises and how they were handled. It is folklore that is handed down to newcomers. Tales are told over whisky and New World wines in the manner of that scene in the movie *Jaws* where old shark bites are revealed and discussed. Here is a sample of five salty seadog account handling tales:

- The pitch team who after a two-hour journey to the client found that they had left the presentation slides back at the agency.
- The 3D direct mail package that caused evacuations of public buildings and controlled explosions by the bomb squad.
- The pornographic attachments that were sent via e-mail by accident to a prudish client.
- Suppliers and agency personnel who wrote to client CEOs telling them what they *really* thought of the agency, client company, life in general etc.

- The finance department that left an A4 piece of paper with all the agency's salaries on the photocopier. (It was replicated by a well-wisher and distributed in the agency's internal post.)

Sometimes these anecdotes are told merely because they are good stories. Don't forget, though, that folklore in tribal gatherings (ancient and modern) is there to provide therapy for those involved and useful lessons for newcomers. My suggestion is to get colleagues to talk about campaign mishaps, discuss how they were handled and start to formulate your own solutions. In this way you practise before the worst happens and you keep your evaluational skills keen.

Information/Depth of Knowledge

In dealing with a critical situation, you will create mere options, make a better decision and be able to prioritize if you are armed with information.

Take a situation where your client wants to change the headline of an ad and you have to tell the creative team that it needs to be changed. You know that you have a problem on your hands when the ad is promoting a pets' retirement home. The client wants to change the headline from 'It's a Dog's Life' to 'Animals Now Don't Need to Take Pot Luck' at the eleventh hour. The image is the classic cartoon of labradors playing pool in a smoky bar.

You think you understand. The retirement home is not just for dogs. The great creative concept has inspired the client to come up with their own headline and this is what they want changed.

In order to deal with a situation like this you need to be a good listener. You are a seasoned pro, so such a last-minute change does not phase you. However, at the moment you have a limited number of options. Before you rush off to the creative department, explore the situation for more information.

Develop Your Questioning Skills

Questioning provides information. It allows you to explore different aspects without seeming to disagree. It buys you time, because you are seen to be considering all the issues and this can be helpful to the other party as well. It also helps you redefine or reframe a problem. And it creates a dialogue rather than confrontation.

- Use open questions to explore the feelings and the background. (Closed questions only elicit a fact or a yes/no answer.)
- Explore reasons in depth. (The stated reasons may not be the real motivation.)
- Analyse whether there are any other issues, pressures or people involved.
- Summarize answers to test your own understanding.
- Develop hypothetical scenarios to test acceptability. ('What if we retouched cats into the pool-playing scene?')

Develop Your Listening Skills

Listening is the complementary skill to questioning. You will receive better answers if the person feels that you are really listening. Also you can develop your listening skills to recognize things that your conversation partner does not necessarily want to impart.

You can improve the effectiveness of your listening by:

- Showing interest/desire to understand (e.g. eye contact, enthusiastic voice, empathetic statements).
- Paying 100% attention.
- Asking questions that clarify and confirm understanding.
- Unearthing the different layers of information (e.g. 'You don't like the headline? I was under the impression you liked it at concept presentation. What has changed in the meantime?' 'I changed my mind.' 'What made you change your mind?' 'A meeting with my boss . . .').
- Listening instinctively (paying attention to body language, tone and sensitivities).
- Taking notes.

If you conduct the information-gathering exercise correctly, it will give you more options and lead you to a better decision. Most importantly, the client feels that they have your attention and you are listening.

COMMENT

In the above case, good listening yielded a totally different situation than originally detected. In fact, the real problem was that the client had shown the visual to the boss, who did not like it. The change of headline was the direct client's idea to placate the boss because he had ended the conversation with 'And for heaven's sake, the retirement home is not just for dogs!'. The account handler at least avoided the next fall (dissatisfaction with the suggested amendments) and in the end the creative team developed a previous concept to the satisfaction of both agency and client.

Timing

In a difficult situation time is normally a very scarce resource. As in more formal situations, J.W. Kaine in his seminar on *Mastering the Art of Advertising Negotiations* (1998) notes that 'negotiation skills are not the forte of advertising executives. . . . As an agency person you are practised at the art of satisfying the client . . . and quickly. A skilful negotiator understands the use of time and is not afraid to use the tactic of forbearance to get what he/she needs.'

Consequently, you need to be prepared to use time differently than in other client–servicing situations.

Let's go back to me in Coney Island at the baseball batting cages (see Figure 5.1). When people playing a sport (like me in an amusement park attraction!) are comfortable with being 'in the zone', they feel that they mentally slow down or speed up the ball according to their style. If it were physically possible, I would want the baseball to appear from the machine really slowly (between points 1 and 2), then it could speed up (between points 2 and 3). Then between points 3 and 4, I would choose which part of the bat I would hit the ball with and then whack it into the roaring crowds. Ideally you would like something similar to happen in the difficult situations you regularly face.

You want the difficult situation to make itself visible slowly so that you can assess the circumstances and make a judgement. Then you want to speed up the process to arrive at closure. And finally, you want it to slow down again so you can check everything is correct.

You cannot literally slow things down, of course. However, you will find that taking your time, assessing your options, discussing the situation with other

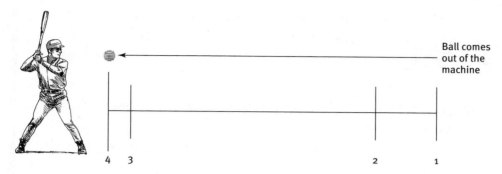

Figure 5.1 At the batting cages

parties and making a considered decision will ultimately save you time in the long run.

How to speed up the process once the decision has been made depends on the problem. Nevertheless, you should be conscious of not throwing caution to the wind in your quality control checks.

The Message

If you have to deliver a message to your supplier, client or partner, you need to control a number of elements. Preparation will help design the content. For example, if you are presenting a problem, it is better to accompany this with a solution or various options. The way it is phrased and the context in which it is delivered are also very important.

We have discussed how information is key to handling a difficult situation. Let us return to the dogs ad headline scenario. Before you can commit to the headline/concept being amended, you need to talk to your creative team. Naturally, if you are negotiating something like this with your client, there will be another negotiation with the internal team. Consequently, if there are two interdependent negotiations, make sure you can rely on the result of the subsidiary negotiation to deliver success in the main negotiation. In the headline example, if you cannot get your team to amend the concept in the next 24 hours, don't start the negotiation on time with the client. Or likewise, if you have to cancel on your partner, don't say you will make it up by taking them to this year's Venice Carnival if you have not investigated flights and availability.

A number of times you will encounter resistance. Here are six ways to deal with resistance recommended by J.W. Kaine in his *Mastering the Art of Advertising Negotiations* seminar (1998):

1   Listen. It is very hard to handle resistance if you don't know what the other person's concerns are.
2   Restate the other negotiator's viewpoint. This confirms to them that you really understand what their concerns are.
3   Ask the other negotiator what they would consider a good solution. There are always good ideas on both sides in a negotiation. This step demonstrates openness on your part and has the added advantage of getting them to reveal their 'bottom line'. You now know what separates you and the other party from an agreement.
4   Ask open questions about their proposal that reveal its weaknesses.
5   When the other side's proposal has been diluted, propose an idea that may answer everybody's concerns.
6   If you must make a concession, make sure that you do it in a way that builds an obligation on their part for the next concession.

The Communications Climate

If it is a difficult situation, the message is going to be tough for the client to hear. Therefore you need to optimize the context/climate. Look at the following elements and see how you can influence them:

- **Medium:** Is face to face better or would a long written letter be preferable (because of the complexity of the problem)? What about a combination?
- **People:** Who should be present at the meeting? Are you looking for allies, experts and friendly faces or it would be better one to one?
- **Timing:** For example, a message delivered at the end of the day adds to the stress of what has gone on before. If you can, wait until the morning to address it.
- **Location:** Neutral territory is often better. A calming atmosphere might be also needed.

- **Phraseology:** Prepare and rehearse in your mind the best way of expressing the message.

COMMENT

Overall, difficult situations are only problematic when we don't pay enough attention to them. Also remember to keep a sense of perspective, needed to evaluate how a message rates in the client's eyes.

In the chapter 'An overview of the pressures on the client' in *Excellence in Advertising* (Butterfield, 1999), Mike Sommers explains the communications climate exquisitely:

Question: You're a client. It's 9.30am on a Friday morning. You've been called out of a board meeting which convened at 7.30am to discuss the extremely poor sales position of the last several weeks. On your way to the phone your secretary uses the opportunity to tell you that the corrective promotion you had hoped to run has been declared illegal, and that the two key executives you needed to see later that morning in order to share the panic are on a buying trip to the Far East. Behind your back your colleagues – you are sure – are using your absence from the room as an opportunity to stress to the Managing Director how much the sales situation is down to your indecisive management style. You pick up the phone, it's the Creative Director of your agency who says, 'Look, I know you were pretty definite with Jeremy, but I just wanted to check if we were right down to the wire on the price issue. We really don't want to put a price flash on tomorrow's ad – we think it's much better if it's left to the reader's imagination. If you could come over and let the creatives explain then we've got the Mirror to delay its deadline on copy – you'll only miss the Northern Ireland edition and the position will be virtually as good as the original negotiation.'
Do you:

1 Suggest the board meeting is postponed due to an important development at the agency?
2 Ring your Account Director suggesting they run the ad as you agreed and stop the Creative Director bothering you?
3 Give everybody at the agency both barrels over the phone and then put a call into the Ad Agency Register?

As you can see, the emotional state of the person you are communicating with is key. Make sure this is gauged correctly.

EXPLOITING EXCELLENT SITUATIONS

This is where you are in that famous 'zone' and you elect to extend your time there. There are two areas of so-called zone extension that I want to highlight: the beginning of relationships and during times of success.

Extending the Honeymoon Period

In all new relationships there is an initial period that is about getting to know each other and anticipating a client's needs (personal and business). It is in the interests of the agency to use this time to surprise and impress the client. My suggestions for this period (in connection with those mentioned in the client relationship section of Chapter 4) are:

- Get to know the client contacts very well and exploit the personal chemistry (social events are very useful for this).
- Understand the client marketplace very quickly and be seen at industry events.
- Promote the agency by sharing other client experiences (use of media etc.) with the new client.
- Demonstrate 'going the extra mile' again and again.
- Brainstorm potential ideas inside the agency and every time there is a client meeting, discuss one killer idea that will add to the client's business.
- Walk the corridors of the client company and secure introductions.

COMMENT

Lester Wunderman, in his enthralling book *Being Direct* (1996), talks about the habit of corridor walking and always having at least one new idea to wow the client with. Obviously not all these ideas will be acted on, but it shows the client that you are thinking about their business all the time. You are keen and hungry and, in the client's eyes, you may be more worthy to be awarded a contract than another agency.

Extending the Success of a Campaign

Imagine you have just launched an advertising campaign that has been phenomenally successful. Here are tips to lengthen the spotlight on your success:

- Identify the elements of the success and come up with a proposal to the client to extend or replicate that success.
- Make other people in the client company aware of the success. Either initiate this yourself or provide the client with the information/material to do it.
- Alert the rest of the agency to the success and congratulate the team.
- Create an internal presentation to promote the success.
- Contact the relevant trade and marketing press for coverage of the story.
- Enter the campaign for awards.

COMMENT

These are such obvious things and yet in 80% of cases only one or two of them are done. If you are in control of your time and space, you should be in a position to achieve these things as a matter of course.

IMPROVING YOUR PRESENTATIONS

There are a number of training courses that deal with giving outstanding presentations. Because account personnel have to give a variety of these (creative concepts, strategic proposals, internal communications), it is a fundamental skill to master.

I will state the principles of presentations and give you tips that can help in an agency environment. However, my recommendation is that you observe expert speakers and note what they do in presentations. For example, record an arts lecture on television or get a video out of a business library (particularly of a speaker trained by one of the big consultancy groups). Look at the principles and see how that presenter tailors them to their own style. If it is someone in your company who you have seen deliver a seminar, discuss with them afterwards how they prepared themselves. Then get someone at a similar level to you and conduct a small workshop on the techniques by replaying the presentation.

Those doing marketing diplomas with live case study presentations should consider building in enough time for three days of rehearsal. A video camera that allows you to see how you have performed (and for your colleagues to comment) is invaluable. It will enhance your content and presentation style immeasurably.

COMMENT

Does this sound a bit raw? A little too exposed? You will do exactly the same sort of exercises at a presentation skills course, but in a more controlled way. My suggestion is if you are not fortunate enough to go on such a course and want to improve without exposing your weaknesses to clients, senior colleagues and so on, this is the only way. Sure, it is a little embarrassing to begin with, but you will start to enjoy the experience when you feel you are learning from it.

Preparing Presentations

1   **What are your objectives?** What do you want people to do or feel at the end of presentation? This will help you design it to focus on the most important elements.
2   **Who is the audience?** This will influence style, format, medium, message and tone. You will need to connect immediately with those in the audience.
3   **Draft the core of your presentation.** Is it clear? Is it too abstract/meandering? Do you need examples, visuals etc.? Share it with someone to get some objective feedback. You can usually cut it by at least 50%. Remember that the time per slide can be roughly two minutes without any questions. Keep charts very simple.
4   **Fine-tune the introduction and conclusion.** Have you set the scene, told the audience why and what you will be presenting? In the conclusion, have you summarized and ended on the points you want them to have their heads?

5 **Prepare notes to help.** Look at each section and be confident about how you are going to introduce it. Know which story you are going to lead with. Write out the first two minutes of the presentation. This is not so you can read it out or speak it off by heart. It is so that you will be comfortable with the ideas that you will be hitting the audience with at the beginning.

6 **Practise and rehearse.** The more you practise, the more comfortable and confident you become.

A few additional tips:

- Make sure that you have secured the best location for the presentation (goldfish-bowl meeting rooms are not good).
- Discourage interruptions and distractions (put a sign on the door, ask people to turn off phones).
- Prepare the ground so that the audience will be in a receptive mood.
- Place the audience in accessible, visible seats.
- Identify what time the audience has, let them know how long it is going to be and be timely (a clock on the wall always helps).
- Have presentation aids (OHPs, creative concepts etc.) at hand and know when and in what order they will be introduced. Also decide beforehand whether handouts will be available during or after the meeting.
- Check lighting, visibility and air conditioning at the beginning and have someone monitor them through the presentation.
- Sit in a client's seat before the meeting to check visibility and put yourself in their place and think what is expected and what the reactions will be.
- Have a list of difficult questions and accompanying answers.
- Psych up yourself and your team. Visualize a successful outcome.
- Frame the meeting so that everyone knows who else is in the room, what they can expect and what their role is.
- Let them know when questions should be asked.
- Concentrate on the beginning. This is the part of the meeting that will set the tone for the rest of the meeting.
- Don't read from slides verbatim.

- Engage the audience with:

  - eye contact
  - questions
  - humour
  - name checks ('Jill, you will recognize this situation').

- Understand who the decision maker is.
- Judge the mood and need for:

  - questions
  - refreshments
  - courtesy breaks
  - active participation.

- Make sure that all issues are addressed.
- Summarize the meeting and the next steps.

COMMENT

Remember the little things. I have heard of a new marketing director coming to an agency for his first presentation. Instead of the usual, very able receptionist, there was a temp. Unfortunately, the temp did not know how important the director was, how important the first meeting was and even how to pronounce the name of the company. The client said he felt as though he were there to be interviewed rather than, as he pointed out, the other way round.

GETTING INVOLVED IN PITCHES

I have found that when it comes to pitches, all the great principles of client servicing, strategic development and presentations seem to head out of the window. Why do reason and sense just vanish? I am not sure whether it is the initial rush of adrenalin, too much caffeine or the prospect of late-night pizzas that brings this on. However, the basic rules still apply even in these super-incubated conditions.

I suggest a return to the fundamental principles so that all is not lost in the flow of adrenalin. Clients still want the following from agencies, as we saw in Chapter 3:

Primary Criteria	Delivery Criteria
Capabilities/resources	Speed to market
World–class people	Quality delivery
Vision	Professionalism
Creativity	Cost efficiencies
Marketplace knowledge	
Sector/media experience	
Partnerships/network	

Whereas with an established client you have the luxury of displaying these factors over a period of time, with a new client you need to demonstrate all of them over a short space of time and also understand how the potential client prioritizes the criteria.

In addition to my recommendations for normal client assessment, project management and presenting effectively, here are a few suggestions for approaching pitches:

1   Ask the client to name the competing agencies (some agencies will not pitch if they don't know them; see point 9).
2   Profile the pitch clients on a personal and business experience level (use contacts to gain knowledge and insight).
3   Create a timing schedule for the pitch and appoint a pitch project manager.
4   Allow a generous time for rehearsal.
5   Institute a mini marketplace competitive review to build knowledge of the sector if this is not available.
6   Understand how the client prioritizes primary and delivery criteria. Show proof points. Construct your presentation accordingly.
7   Construct a pitch team with good internal and outward-facing chemistry.
8   In terms of timing, don't synchronize strategy development and creative development. Accelerate strategy development to feed into creative development.
9   Review your pitch presentation for its competitive edge (against your knowledge of other competing agencies).
10   Exploit any meetings with clients.
11   Review your presentation with a tame client if possible or with selected colleagues.

12 Emphasize the people who will be working on the client's business.

13 Optimize the creative side – it is the essential expression of the agency.

14 Go further (in terms of quality) with visual aids.

15 Get the team to bond and psych themselves up well in advance of the pitch.

16 Rehearse, rehearse, rehearse.

17 Check printers, photocopiers, paper stocks, network memory space – well in advance.

18 Don't add timings, costs and metrics merely as afterthoughts.

19 Control the reception and meeting room environment.

20 Demonstrate enthusiasm, passion and hunger for the business.

TIP

I'm sure if you spoke to seasoned new business professionals they would come up with more tips, but here's another way of looking at the pitch:

You are a client seeing four agencies in one week. This means some heavy presentations with people whom you don't know but who treat you reverentially. You work out with your colleagues a scoring system that is weighted to your priorities (see the previous decision matrices in Chapter 1).

You are not the main decision maker, but you will be working with the agency every day, therefore you will resent any agency that just pitches at the 'big cheese'.

You are interested in the people and how they work together in the presentation, as it will be indicative of a future relationship.

You see the same sort of thing in each pitch, as agencies can be quite unimaginative in their presentations.

After the pitch, even though only one agency has been selected, you were very impressed by another agency and would be happy to work with them in another situation.

In other words, think about all the factors from the client's standpoint.

COMMENT

Remember, stuff happens and sometimes you can prevent it, other times you can't. Sympathize with the agency whose new business prospect discovered his claustrophobia on the way up to the agency by getting stuck in a lift for 45 minutes. Suffice to say, he did not take the conversation further.

EXERCISES

1   List your last three difficult situations with colleagues and detail the events from your point of view and another's point of view. Suggest improvements from the two points of view.

2   List the people in the agency with whom it would pay to have a good relationship.

3   Name your most successful presentation. Analyse why it was rewarding.

LOOKING AFTER YOURSELF

CHAPTER 6

LOOKING AFTER YOURSELF

In this chapter you will learn about:

- Being the master of your own destiny.

- Setting your own goals.

- Enhancing your performance appraisal process.

- How an agency can maximize personal career development.

This chapter is really about personal development. Agency environments are so fast moving that one moment you are concentrating on an account and the next time you look up, a year has gone by. When you have holidays all you want to do is switch off from work and enjoy the moment. And why not? You deserve it. Yet if you don't watch out, you can easily get lost in the complexities of work and forget why you started in the first place. This chapter deals with individuals and agencies taking a step back and creating a long-term overview for individual development. It tackles how an individual can look after No. 1 and how agencies can look after their most precious resource – their people.

BEING THE MASTER OF YOUR OWN DESTINY

You will have to excuse me for the next few minutes, as I am going to become morbid. This is only to prove a point and make you think about your career differently.

Scenario 1

It is a Thursday evening and after a hard day at the office you decide to leave relatively early. You put your coat on, say good night to your colleagues and walk out of the agency. You reach the high street and are walking across the road to the newsagent's when the proverbial double-decker bus comes by, runs you over and kills you. In this hypothetical situation, let me put a few questions to you. Is this the occupation you thought you would have in your obituary? Did you achieve the things you wanted to in the last few years? Will graveside eulogies describe you as successful and fulfilled? Who would attend the funeral?

Let's be more positive and use the theatrical technique employed in the Gwyneth Paltrow film *Sliding Doors*. The film follows the heroine in two situations – one where she misses catching an underground train and the other where she does not. Both situations create different consequences.

Scenario 2

As in the other scenario, you put on your coat, say goodnight and walk out of the agency. You reach the high street and are walking across the road to the newsagent's when the same double-decker bus screeches to a halt with you in front of it. The bus driver is screaming at you about the potential fatality. You are visibly shaken, but having been so wrapped up in your thoughts, you don't really appreciate how near those graveside eulogies you came. In the second situation you have a lucky reprieve, although you don't recognize it as such. Maybe if you did, you would approach things differently.

I have described both scenarios in the context of work, but really I am broadening the subject of personal development to all areas of your life. I am highlighting the themes of success, fulfilment and happiness here, as I think it is important that we don't drift though work without a good idea of what we are trying to achieve on a personal basis. It will allow you when you have those moments of reflection to know whether you are on track or not – it will help you strive for the next goal.

It is up to each of us to define our own success and happiness. Yet there are obvious benefits:

1   We know where we are going.
2   We know why we are doing things.
3   We can articulate what we want.
4   People understand us clearly.
5   It reduces the number of things that just 'happen' to us.
6   We become more confident.
7   We are happier.
8   We can help people.
9   It gives us a better understanding of people and their actions.
10   Our lives have a context.

These apply to our work lives as much as to our personal lives.

COMMENT

In 1955 those on the leadership program at Harvard Business School were asked how many of them had a life plan: 3% said they had.

In 1985, the School surveyed the same people to see what had happened in the intervening 30 years. The aggregate wealth of the 3% exceeded the aggregate wealth of the 97%. Not only that, the 3% were happier, fitter, healthier and had fewer divorces than the 97%.

What is interesting about defining success or self-fulfilment is that there is no standard definition. Sure, the terms encapsulate a set of paradigms and experiences, a cocktail of ambitions and reality. Yet these are evaluated differently according to the individual. Each individual sets their own definition.

There is a plethora of self-development books, courses and philosophies to help you understand what is right for you. I found Chérie Carter-Scott's

Table 6.1   Rules for success

Rule One
EACH PERSON HAS THEIR OWN DEFINITION OF SUCCESS
There is no universal definition of success. Everyone has their individual vision of what it means to be fulfilled

Rule Two
WANTING SUCCESS IS THE FIRST STEP TOWARDS ATTAINING IT
When you experience the initial spark of desire, you set the game of success in motion

Rule Three
SELF-TRUST IS ESSENTIAL
To be fulfilled, you must know yourself and honour your truth

Rule Four
GOALS ARE THE STEPPING-STONES ON YOUR PATH
Your journey to fulfilment is propelled forward by the goals you set along the way

Rule Five
YOUR ACTIONS AFFECT YOUR OUTCOMES
The quantity and quality of your energy you put forth directly impacts the results you receive

Rule Six
OPPORTUNITIES WILL BE PRESENTED
There will be moments in life when you are presented with new options. What you choose in those moments is up to you

Rule Seven
EACH SETBACK PROVIDES VALUABLE LESSONS
There will be disappointments and perceived failures along the way. Learning from these experiences offers you precious insight that can lead you to future success

Rule Eight
MANAGING YOUR RESOURCES MAXIMIZES YOUR EFFORTS
Your time, energy, relationships and finances are your most valuable assets. Handling them wisely enhances your ability to succeed

Rule Nine
EVERY LEVEL OF SUCCESS BRINGS NEW CHALLENGES
Each accomplishment alters your reality, either slightly or dramatically. Your task is to maintain your balance when your game board shifts

Rule Ten
SUCCESS IS A PROCESS THAT NEVER ENDS
Each plateau has a new ascent. Once you reach the top, there is a new peak to embrace

Source: Extract from *If Success Is a Game, These Are the Rules* (by Chérie Carter-Scott published by Vermilion. Used by permission of The Random House Group Limited.)

book *If Success Is a Game, These Are the Rules* (2000) a good summary for understanding this territory (see Table 6.1).

SETTING YOUR OWN GOALS

I will focus on goal setting, as mentioned in Rule Four, to help you understand how you can steer your personal development in an agency context.

One of the most important steps to effective goal setting is starting with the endgame in mind. It is a simple idea that will help you immeasurably. If you don't know where you are going, you won't know whether you are on the right road.

TIP

The following technique has been recommended by a number of self-development authors to help focus your thinking. I return to our double-decker accident. Imagine yourself in a dream, at a crowded funeral service. You walk up the corridor to pay your respects to the deceased. You look into the coffin and it is, in fact, your dead body. You take a place to hear the eulogies. There are representatives from your family, friends and work. Each representative describes what you were like in that particular context. What would you expect them to say about your character, habits and achievements? What anecdotes would they use to prove their point?

Take your time to do this. Sit down in peace and quiet and visualize the scene. Then write down what people would say.

If you have been honest, explore any discrepancy between what they would say and what you would have wanted them to say.

The above tip of visualizing your own funeral is a good way to kick off your thinking about how you wish to be known. This will start to build an understanding of what you would like to achieve and be known for. However, I would be deceiving you if I said that this alone will enlighten you as to what you should be heading for. If you have chance, read Stephen Covey's excellent *The 7 Habits of Highly Effective People* (1992). It will definitely charge you with inspired thinking. It will help you think about a personal mission statement, your own vision (business and personal) and the goals that will help you express and achieve these.

When it comes to goal setting for personal development in a work context, don't forget that goals need to follow the same rules as the marketing goals your client sets (Table 6.2).

Table 6.2   Goals need to be SMART

Specific	Goals need to be clear and articulate what is expected in terms of what, by when, where and by how much.
Measurable	If you can't measure a goal, you won't know whether you have achieved it.
Achievable	Goals need to be realistic. They can be slightly aspirational, but definitely achievable. This will maintain motivation.
Relevant	Goals need to relate correctly to the overall vision so that the latter can be achieved.
Time related	There must be starting and ending points so that those involved are aware of time constraints.

If you are formulating goals that you want to be judged by other people in addition to yourself, you may wish to bear the following in mind.

- Discuss the goal setting (for example at your personal appraisal) with those people you want to be evaluated by (e.g. your boss, department head).
- Be clearly in agreement on what the goals entail.
- The other parties should be aware of the SMART elements of the goals.
- Pick goals that have the greatest relevance to your team, account group, agency.
- Simple goals are best.
- Select two or three goals that will have the most impact.
- Set a time by which these goals are going to be evaluated.
- Review your goals regularly. Keep the list at the bottom of your in-tray or put it in your electronic diary so that the goals pop up every week/month.

ENHANCING YOUR PERFORMANCE APPRAISAL PROCESS

COMMENT

Jane was a senior account manager in a large agency and was keen to become an account director. She worked very hard and so did her boss, Rachel, a group account director. In fact, Rachel seemed to be always out of the office with client commitments abroad and out of London. When it came to Jane's appraisal, it was a series of disasters. It was postponed three times. When it did happen, no meeting room had been booked so it was conducted in Rachel's office (with the usual interruptions) and Rachel had only allotted an hour. Consequently the appraisal had to be resumed at a later date. Preparation was minimal and ultimately the outcome for Jane was unsatisfactory.

This kind of story is common. A good deal of problems can be laid at the door of the appraiser. However, if you see yourself as the master of your own destiny, you, as the appraisee, will need to make sure that such problems do not occur. You have to be selfish about such things or events will just take over.

I remember the actor Jeremy Irons on a radio chat show explaining his own such revelation as a young out-of-work actor doing gardening to pay the bills. He realized that he was ultimately the only one who was worried about his career. He could stay a gardener or become a successful actor. Because he wanted to be the latter so much, he made it happen for himself. OK, luck and timing always help, but don't rely on other people to look out for your future. There are too many distractions for other people.

Similarly, Jane could not rely on Rachel to look out for her career advancement, however much it should have been Rachel's responsibility.

Pitiful though it might be, be aware of the reality in certain agencies. When it comes to taking responsibility for your personal appraisal, think about the following:

1   Take the time to prepare for the meeting.
2   Assess your performance against your job description.
3   Make sure your assessor has:

   –   Booked a suitable meeting room.
   –   Allocated sufficient time.
   –   Spoken to the right sources for balanced feedback.
   –   Reviewed your previously agreed action plan.

4   Decide with your assessor about a secondary assessor (this broadens relationships and does not allow you to become dependent on one person above you).

5   Prepare a list of examples to demonstrate your achievements. (Align these closely with account/agency goals.)

6   Determine what you would like your future action plan to be. (Align it with your own personal goals.)

7   Identify anything else you wish to comment on. Don't forget supporting evidence for this.

8   If it is the right time and you are comfortable, ask if you can talk about a salary rise in a separate meeting. Elsewhere, give an indication of what you are expecting and why. Don't get involved in a longer conversation about this.

TIP

If you want to be high profile in your performance improvement so that it will be recognized in your next appraisal, ensure the desired outcome through the following:

- Behaviour/attitude (results, reliability, proactivity, keenness etc.).
- Tone of communication.
- Interpersonal relationships (clients, assessor(s), colleagues).
- Speech/written work.
- Dress.

HOW AN AGENCY CAN MAXIMIZE PERSONAL CAREER DEVELOPMENT

In these times of scarce skilled account handlers, there is a good deal of lip service paid to an agency's workforce. Because of this, it has become a rather cynical cliché that people are an agency's greatest asset. Well, they are! Moreover, agencies need to start understanding how to develop and maximize the potential within their asset.

What I am talking about here is organizational or personal performance management. This is often ignored as a formal practice by agencies. Some agencies don't feel they have the time for such practices; others believe that they should not be investing in this because ultimately when the employee moves on, somebody else will benefit and they will be left having to start again. To me, the latter argument sounds like people who refuse to own pets because they ultimately die.

As Brian Watling identifies in his book *The Appraisal Checklist*, (2000), performance management has the characteristics described in Table 6.3.

Table 6.3   Performance management characteristics

- Keeps the (organizational) vision focused and in place.
- Sets performance standards and objectives across the organization.
- Offers two-way feedback on performance and issues.
- Identifies training and development needs.
- Strengthens and builds relationships.
- Maximizes people potential.
- Can provide a database of people skills for succession planning.
- Keeps the organization competitive.
- Aids morale (only when meaningful).

Source: Brian Watling, *The Appraisal Checklist*; reproduced by permission of Pearson Education Limited.

Those responsible for managing the performance of an account handling department should make sure that they are rigorous in completing all the stages as described in Figure 6.1 and the rest of the section.

Stage 1

Effective performance management allows the mission and vision to permeate throughout the agency and all personal goals to be aligned with these. Consequently, the agency's values, objectives, mission and strategy need to be agreed and transparent to everyone.

For example, an imaginary digital media company, WDGW Agency, might have the following:

Agency values:	Imaginative, having integrity, experimental
Agency mission:	To partner blue-chip clients in the arena of digital strategy and implementation
Agency objectives:	To grow existing business by 20%
(Year X)	To bring in $1m income in new business
	To maintain client satisfaction of 92%
	To explore the future impact of the new converging technologies

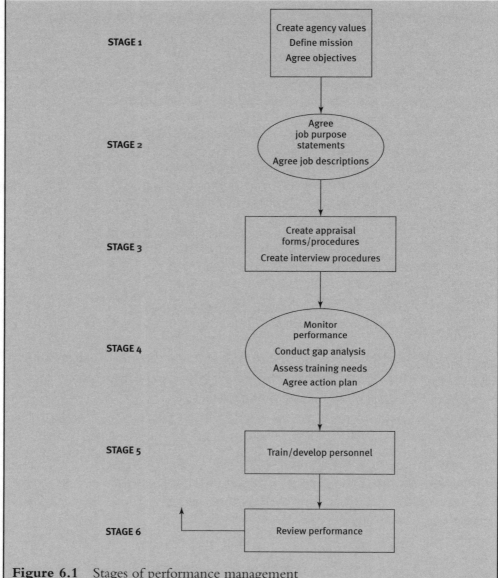

Figure 6.1 Stages of performance management

Stage 2

Job purpose statements and job descriptions are interlinked. Ideally, a candidate or employee should understand the essence of their job through the job purpose and what they have to do in detail through the job description. Let's remind ourselves of the account manager position in Chapter 1 (Figure 1.2). The job purpose would be:

To assist in the client servicing of Donky Cars for We Do Great Work, delivering digital strategy/campaigns to high satisfaction standards.

This short statement, linking into the agency mission statement, allows the candidate/employee to understand what is expected of them and how they will be assessed.

The job description helps qualify the:

- Area of responsibility.
- Skills set needed and at what level the skills are required.
- Reporting structure.
- Remuneration package.

Stage 3

We have discussed interviewing forms and procedures. Here I will concentrate on the appraisal form and procedures.

Appraising personal development should be continuous but, in terms of formal reviews, I would recommend six-monthly assessments. The reason for this is that agencies and accounts are fast-moving environments. I would also recommend that employee and employer mark in their diary quarterly milestones to monitor: 'How are we doing on the development plan?'

A salary review tends to be linked to one performance review. That is not a problem as long as performance and salary reviews are not discussed at the same time in the same meeting. This can create mixed messages.

As an appraiser, you need to pay good attention to:

- Setting up the appraisal.
- Receiving feedback on performance to date.
- Having the right paperwork for the appraisal:

  - Personal development plan agreed at last appraisal.
  - Performance feedback sources.

Job Description: Account Manager

Role and Responsibilities
- Assist Account Director in development and implementation of account and major campaigns
- Liaise with central client on campaigns
- Run singlehandedly minor digital campaigns to satisfaction of client
- Maintain account admin (including client correspondence and finances)
- Liaise with other European market clients on translation activity for campaigns
- Coordinate with project management and creative department to deliver client campaigns
- Supervise outside suppliers and partners
- Create and maintain project files and creative guard book
- Manage Account Administrator

Skill Set Required
- Good digital campaign management skills
- Pan-European coordination experience essential
- Languages an asset (preferably French)
- Good admin and project management skills
- Potential to manage team members
- Feels comfortable with sophisticated creative products

Technical Knowledge/Processes
- Agency campaign process
- Agency intranet usage

Personality Traits/Skills
- Outgoing, confident, flexible
- Good at building relationships (face to face and virtual)
- Good communication skills
- Enjoys challenges
- Enthusiastic, committed and passionate

Remuneration
- Salary $xxk
- Annual agency-wide bonus
- Health cover
- Life cover (4 times annual salary at employment)
- Company pension scheme

Figure 6.2 Sample account manager job description

- – Skills assessment.
- – Technical knowledge/process assessment.
- Conducting the appraisal, including:

  - – Appraisee self-evaluation.
  - – Factors beyond the control of the individual affecting performance.
  - – Development needs and aspirations.
  - – Understanding the gap between performance and desired performance.

- Conducting a follow-up meeting, including:

  - – Confirming personal development plan.
  - – Appraisee's comments on appraisal.

- Forwarding signed appraisal to personnel files.

Setting up the Appraisal

- Book a specific meeting room (not a 'goldfish bowl')
- Allot enough time (two hours plus 30 minutes for a follow-up meeting).
- Don't cancel or postpone.
- Don't allow interruptions.

Receiving Feedback on Performance to Date

There are a number of sources that will help you understand how the appraisee is performing. The individual situation will determine how much importance you attach to each source. Whatever applies, you should impress the importance of discretion and confidentiality on those you talk to.

The following sources are useful:

- Personal observation of performance (in action, meetings, presentations, written work).
- Client feedback.
- Team feedback.
- Other departmental feedback.
- Client satisfaction surveys.

Conducting the Appraisal

In terms of structuring the appraisal, think about the following:

- At the beginning, put the appraisee at ease and explain the process and objectives of the appraisal.
- Personally, I favour appraisals with a secondary assessor. However, you and the appraisee need to decide what is more appropriate.
- The appraisal form should be used as a checklist for the areas to be discussed, but make sure that you allow free-flow conversation and response to the feedback.
- The appraisee should be able to:

  - Give their evaluation of their performance.
  - Describe the factors beyond their control that have affected performance.
  - Explore development needs and future aspirations.
  - Identify their proposals for their personal development action plan.

- In giving feedback, the appraiser should be aware of Brian Watling's 8 Golden Rules of Feedback and Evaluation (Table 6.4).

Table 6.4   8 Golden Rules of Feedback and Evaluation

1	Avoid feeding back on what it should have been.
2	Do not speak jargon.
3	Avoid feedback based just on opinion.
4	Keep the feedback/evaluation relevant.
5	Limit feedback to something that can be actioned.
6	Avoid criticism.
7	Do be specific.
8	Watch out for overkill.

Source: Brian Watling, *The Appraisal Checklist*; reproduced by permission of Pearson Education Limited.

COMMENT

Remember, performance management can be and sound a little automaton-like. What we are dealing with here are people's career dreams, personal traits and work relationships/friendships. Be sensitive to how what you say comes over and be cautious as to where you tread.

STRICTLY CONFIDENTIAL
PERSONAL PERFORMANCE
APPRAISAL FORM

Name of Employee: _____

Title: _____

Reviewed by: _____

Secondary Assessor: _____

Date: _____

For period covering: _____

Signed after 2nd stage:

Primary Assessor _____ Date _____

Secondary Assessor _____ Date _____

Appraisee _____ Date _____

Performance Appraisal Steps

- Manager initiates the process, scheduling an appraisal with appraisee.
- At the time meeting is scheduled, the employee should receive a blank copy of the evaluation form (all parts) and previous form.
- The employee completes Part 1 (Specific Performance Assessment) and Part 2 (the Self-Appraisal Form).
- The Primary Assessor should consult with all appropriate people. This will enable the Assessor to give a complete picture of the Appraisee.
- The Primary Assessor completes Part 1 (Specific Performance Assessment) and Part 4 (Performance Summary), using the employee's job description to identify key responsibilities.
- Part 1 is completed by both parties prior to the evaluation and scoring agreed in the appraisal.
- Secondary Assessor attends appraisal and completes Part 3.
- Primary Assessor and Appraise discuss Part 5 (Personal Development Plan).
- Both parties reconvene to confirm Personal Development Plan and sign appraisal form.

RATINGS:

Excellent:	Performance is outstanding
Good:	Performance is beyond expected job requirements
Average:	Performance meets basic job requirements and/or may require minor improvement
Needs improving:	Performance is unsatisfactory. Requires immediate action
Not applicable:	Factor not ordinarily called for in particular job, or insufficient time on job to judge

Figure 6.3 Sample appraisal form. (Original source: Wunderman Cato Johnson, London, 2000)

PART 1–Specific Performance Assessment

We Do Great Work
A G E N C Y

	Excellent	Good	Average	Needs improving	Not applicable

1. Achievement Orientation
- Contributes in ways that add value to client's business
- Strives to do best job possible
- Manages projects efficiently
- Understands job description
- Takes action to address personal development needs

2. Initiative
- Anticipates problems and takes actions to avoid or solve them
- Actively seeks and takes on additional responsibility without being asked to do so
- Sets goals and standards that exceed job requirements
- Looks for opportunities to apply prior learning
- Identifies income-generating opportunities and develops them
- Contributes to agency generally

3. Confidence
- Expresses a high degree of confidence in own ability to do the job
- Clients have a high degree of confidence in ability

4. Assertiveness
- Takes firm position to promote the agency's work
- Readily accepts leadership role in situations where it is needed
- Expresses opinions, points of view in constructive manner
- Addresses problems or conflicts directly with others

5. Client Orientation
- Makes extraordinary efforts to learn about the client's business, products and services
- Listens for and helps to elicit key client interests, needs, concerns
- Develops working relationships with key client contacts
- Understands the perspective of the client when evaluating the agency product
- Maximizes the use of agency resources to address client's needs
- Derives strong personal satisfaction from making contributions to client's business

6. Commitment
- Demonstrates strong enthusiasm for and commitment to own job and agency product
- Acts with a sense of urgency to get things done
- Sustains enthusiasm and commitment, even when things are not going well
- Shows commitment to team

Continued overleaf

Figure 6.3   *(continued)*

PART 1–Specific Performance Assessment (Cont.)

We Do Great Work
A G E N C Y

	Excellent	Good	Average	Needs improving	Not applicable
7 Creative Focus					
• Actively participates in creative development process	◯	◯	◯	◯	◯
• Makes sure that creative team has a complete understanding of the product/brief	◯	◯	◯	◯	◯
• Inspires creative team to high standard	◯	◯	◯	◯	◯
8 Specific Expertise					
• Understanding of creative	◯	◯	◯	◯	◯
• People management skills	◯	◯	◯	◯	◯
• Presentation skills	◯	◯	◯	◯	◯
• Day-to-day communication skills	◯	◯	◯	◯	◯
• Personal time management	◯	◯	◯	◯	◯
• Delegation skills	◯	◯	◯	◯	◯
• Listening skills	◯	◯	◯	◯	◯
• Project management skills	◯	◯	◯	◯	◯
• Media knowledge	◯	◯	◯	◯	◯
• Data knowledge	◯	◯	◯	◯	◯
• Interactive knowledge	◯	◯	◯	◯	◯
• Print and production knowledge	◯	◯	◯	◯	◯
• Mailing production knowledge	◯	◯	◯	◯	◯
• Account finances	◯	◯	◯	◯	◯
• Liaison with other agencies	◯	◯	◯	◯	◯
9 Account Admin Skills					
• Understands and implements account procedures	◯	◯	◯	◯	◯
• Keeps filing up-to-date	◯	◯	◯	◯	◯
• Issues contact reports within 24 hours	◯	◯	◯	◯	◯
• Submits estimates and timing plans for all projects	◯	◯	◯	◯	◯
• Masters invoicing procedures	◯	◯	◯	◯	◯
• WP skills	◯	◯	◯	◯	◯

Those who have been consulted in the assessment:

Client Services Director ◯	Creative Director ◯	Creative Services ◯
Planning ◯	Finance Director ◯	Client ◯
Other(s):		

Factors out of individual's control to be considered during performance appraisal? (please state):

Figure 6.3   *(continued)*

PART 2–Self-Appraisal Form

We Do Great Work
A G E N C Y

The purpose of this form is to help both you and your manager get the most benefit from your appraisal interview. Please look at the following questions beforehand and, if you wish, make a note of all your answers in the space provided; these will form a valuable basis for discussion during the appraisal.

1 What have been your contributions and achievements during the last six months?

2 What skills and abilities do you believe you bring to the job?

3 What particular skills and abilities do you have that are not being made use of in your current role?

4 In which aspects of your job do you feel you need more experience/guidance/training?

5a Which parts of your job interest you most?

5b Which parts of your job interest you least?

6 In order to improve your job performance, what changes could be made by:
    a Your manager?

    b Yourself?

    c Other people?

7 Any other comments?

Figure 6.3   (*continued*)

Figure 6.3 (*continued*)

PART 4 – Summary of personal performance appraisal

We Do Great Work
A G E N C Y

KEY RESPONSIBILITIES	PERFORMANCE ASSESSMENT

Figure 6.3   *(continued)*

PART 5 – Personal Development Plan

We Do Great Work
A G E N C Y

OBJECTIVES

METHOD

TIMEFRAME

POTENTIAL EVIDENCE?

Figure 6.3   (*continued*)

There are different schools of appraisal processes, with 360-degree feedback becoming more popular, but Figure 6.3 shows a sample of one that I have used in the past.

After the Appraisal

Following the main performance appraisal, allow a 24-hour 'sleep on it' period, then reconvene to confirm and agree the personal development action plan. It is also at this point that you can request the appraisee's opinion on how the appraisal was conducted. Any other comments can be added and then both parties should sign the form, retaining copies for continual monitoring of the action plan and sending one to the personnel files.

EXERCISES

1   Write a profile of yourself that will appear in *Campaign* this year and another one for five years' time.

2   Do you have a job description? (If not, ask your supervisor for one.) Construct your job purpose statement and show it to your boss.

3   Complete Part 5 of the sample performance appraisal form for yourself.

TAKING CARE OF THE FINANCES

CHAPTER 7

TAKING CARE OF THE FINANCES

In this chapter you will learn about:

- The principles of running campaigns cost-effectively.
- Understanding a campaign financial report.
- Understanding an account's financial metrics.
- Budgeting and forecasting.

With all the complexities of a campaign, you can easily concentrate on the strategy and implementation and ignore the financial implications of your decisions. Costs are an integral part of a campaign and ultimately they will catch up with you. It is thus essential to master the discipline.

THE PRINCIPLES OF RUNNING CAMPAIGNS COST-EFFECTIVELY

The different financial stages of a campaign are as follows:

- Campaign budgeting.
- Securing costs from third parties.

- Preparing an estimate.
- Monitoring costs.
- Invoicing the client.
- Preparing a final reconciliation.

I will go through each stage (except reconciliation, which is discussed later), but you may wish to consider the guiding principles that should influence all your financial transactions:

1 **Efficient administration.** If you discipline yourself to record all costs to the client from internal department/third-party suppliers and centralize your records, you will save yourself and others a good deal of time, money and energy.

2 **Comprehensive overview.** A good manager will always need 'helicopter' vision; in other words, the ability to see things from some distance and understand the big picture. When it comes to costs it is necessary to see how individual costs are interdependent; what cost implications (such as amendments) certain decisions have; and whether the overall budget total is being jeopardized.

3 **Client transparency.** Some clients want to know the intricacies of campaign costs; others leave that up to the account team. In fact, some clients have the contractual right to audit your financial records. I have found that the best discipline for an account team is to assume that the financial records will be audited. Consequently, if each individual cost amendment does not need to be documented on an invoice, for example, it still can be seen in any back-up if requested.

4 **Financial embassy.** Costs often become the focus of the client's expression of satisfaction/dissatisfaction with the agency. Therefore in your dealings with the client you have to realize that you and your financial correspondence are ambassadors for the agency. As in real-life embassies, you and your financial 'missives' need to display the appropriate diplomacy. More on this later.

5 **Expectation management.** This is an area of account handling where shocks and surprises are particularly unwelcome. Exercise your communication skills to keep the client informed of where the campaign stands financially on a regular basis.

Campaign Budgeting

Campaign budgeting is defining the total pot of money needed to execute a campaign. The budget will then be broken down into the various campaign cost elements (see Figure 7.1).

If you have created this type of communication before, you will be well qualified to assess what the repeat costs will be. However, there are a number of times (including pitches) where you will have to make informed guesses on future, previously unexecuted campaigns. Submitting an inaccurate cost may lay you open to future problems. Yet not submitting anything is either not an option or, in the case of a pitch, will not get you into the frame. Experience of different scenarios and clients' reactions will help. Nevertheless, if you are new to this I would suggest the following.

Gain some understanding of what the budget holder is prepared to spend. This is a two-edged sword. On the one hand it is worth knowing if the client already has a figure in mind, as you will need to be aware of this when budgeting. On the other hand, if you press them on the subject, you may end up with an unworkable figure that is too low and set yourself up for causing the client disappointment.

No client has an endless pot of money; it is more that they haven't had time to think about it or where else the money could come from. The following questions may help you elicit a considered response from the client:

- Have there been campaigns similar to this (maybe not in terms of mechanics, but in terms of scale in the mind of the client)?
- What are the business and sales objectives?
- Does the client organization work on an allowable market cost per sale/enquiry? For example, they may not have used web banner ads before, but how much does it cost to get the target audience to respond to a call to action in other media (such as ringing a telephone number after reading a press ad)?

Less experienced clients will try to avoid the issue of the budget if they have not thought about it. If you dig deeper, as long as it does not aggravate the client, you may save yourself a good deal of time.

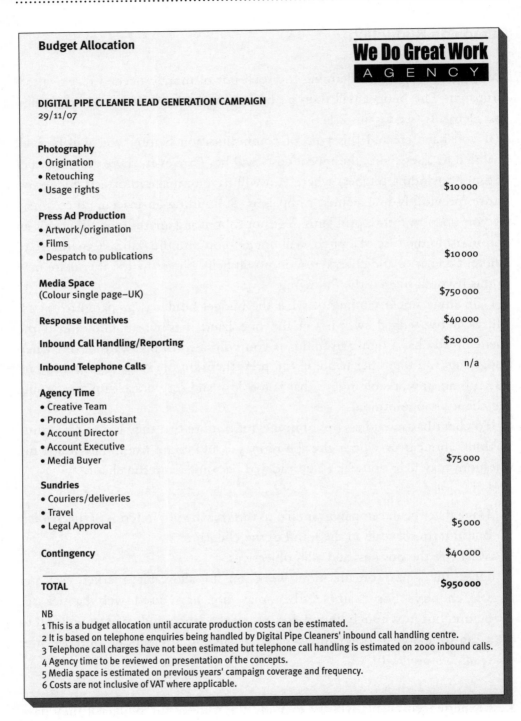

Budget Allocation

We Do Great Work
A G E N C Y

DIGITAL PIPE CLEANER LEAD GENERATION CAMPAIGN
29/11/07

Photography
• Origination
• Retouching
• Usage rights $10 000

Press Ad Production
• Artwork/origination
• Films
• Despatch to publications $10 000

Media Space
(Colour single page–UK) $750 000

Response Incentives $40 000

Inbound Call Handling/Reporting $20 000

Inbound Telephone Calls   n/a

Agency Time
• Creative Team
• Production Assistant
• Account Director
• Account Executive
• Media Buyer $75 000

Sundries
• Couriers/deliveries
• Travel
• Legal Approval $5 000

Contingency $40 000

TOTAL $950 000

NB
1 This is a budget allocation until accurate production costs can be estimated.
2 It is based on telephone enquiries being handled by Digital Pipe Cleaners' inbound call handling centre.
3 Telephone call charges have not been estimated but telephone call handling is estimated on 2000 inbound calls.
4 Agency time to be reviewed on presentation of the concepts.
5 Media space is estimated on previous years' campaign coverage and frequency.
6 Costs are not inclusive of VAT where applicable.

Figure 7.1 Sample budget allocation

Frame any budget/estimate with the fact that it is an informed 'guesstimate' because of the lack of known facts.

You will need to understand how agency costs and third-party costs will be presented to the client. You can either refer to your agency/client agreement or you need to make a separate decision (in consultation with your finance director or your client) on how to structure the costs. For example, here are different ways to work with the client company:

Agency X $10 000 (agency time) + $50 000 (production costs)
          + $0 (agency mark–up) = $60 000

Agency Y $0 (agency time) + $50 000 (production costs)
          + $7500 (15% agency mark–up) = $57 500

Agency Z $5000 (creative fee only) + $50 000 (production costs)
          + $2500 (5% agency mark–up) = $57 500

If you look at this example, you will have differing views as to which arrangement is best (depending on whether you are a client or an agency). However, this is just one example. Think about if the production costs were $5 million. Agency Y's 15% would be $0.75 million! You can only really understand whether this is a good or a bad deal if you know what agency costs you are covering – something to consider when structuring an agreement.

COMMENT

I am in full agreement with the current trend of external costs not being marked up and agencies charging their time based on an hourly rate tariff. It means that in billing terms external costs remain transparent, clients do not think you are inflating internal costs with mark-up, and the account handler can concentrate on covering time spent on the campaign.

Other suggestions include:

- Assess the accuracy of the budget/estimate and use a contingency to safeguard yourself against any shortfall.
- Explore comprehensively all costs involved. Decide whether clients are expecting them to be included (for example, in a sales lead–generation campaign where the response medium is handled by the in-house telephone centre, does the call handling need to be costed?).

- Incorporate into the budget/forecast any provisos, assumptions that help the costs become transparent.

TIPS

1 If you put the agency time further down the budget/estimate, it is not the first thing commented on by the client and you, as an account handler, feel less defensive.
2 Budgets should be explained face to face.
3 Once the client is happy with the budget, ask them to sign it off for your records.

Securing Costs from Third Parties

Whether you are dealing with third parties directly or through your creative services department, I would recommend the following in relation to securing costs:

- Put instructions in writing and keep a record of all correspondence.
- Allow the third party to see the overall picture (including campaign and business objectives).
- Request a full breakdown cost estimate (if you don't, you can bet that your client/boss will) and timing schedule (weekend work may mean extra costs).
- Go to three suppliers (if possible) to ensure competitiveness.
- Don't choose a supplier on cost alone.

Preparing an Estimate

An estimate is a more accurate summary of potential campaign costs than a budget (see Figure 7.2). In creative campaigns, it tends to be presented on approval of the creative concepts.

Think about the following:

- Is the estimate on agency letterhead/according to the agency template?
- Are the job name, job number and date included?

Cost Estimate

We Do Great Work
A G E N C Y

Client:	Digital Pipe Cleaners
Job Title:	Quarter 1 Lead Generation Campaign
Job No.:	DPC 01N 7777
Date:	10/12/07 – Estimate No. 1
Prepared by:	Michael Sims

Photography
- Photographer's fee (see attachment) $3000
- Model fees/set building $5000
- Retouching $1000
- Usage rights $1000

$10000

Press Ad Production
(see media schedule 9/12/07)
- A4 colour version $6000
- DPS colour version $6000
- Despatch to publications $1000

$13000

Media Space
(see schedule 9/12/07)

$750000

Response Incentives
- 3000 @ $10 $30000
- Delivery $1000

$31000

Inbound Response Handling
(as quoted by J. Soap of DPC call handling centre – see email 8/12/07 based on 2000 calls) $40000

Agency Time
- Creative $20000
- Account handling $30000
- Production $10000
- Media $15000

$75000

Legal Approval

$500

Purchase of new freephone number

$5000

Sundries
- Couriers/deliveries
- Internal comms materials

$5000

Contingency

$10500

TOTAL

$940000

NB
1 This estimate does not include VAT where applicable.
2 Any amendments/additions will be communicated accordingly.
3 Third-party supplier costs cannot be approved until this estimate is approved.

Figure 7.2   Sample cost estimate

- Do you need to follow a particular format/procedure at the client's request (inclusion of client purchase order number, job/department reference)?
- Make sure that you keep a copy of the estimate and that you receive a signature on it as proof of approval.

COMMENT

Many people are not comfortable with dealing with costs. Clients become very nervous talking about them. In a way this is understandable, because even the smallest campaign cost is a very significant amount in personal terms and there can be internal ramifications if a marketing person is not seen to be managing their budgets. Therefore a representative of the agency always needs to bear this in mind and also be aware of their ambassadorial role.

At this stage, diplomacy starts with deciding when to present the estimate. An estimate is an expression of intent. Therefore you need to secure the client's confidence in your intent before you present the estimate to them. For example, in the meeting, I would first and foremost present the media schedule and the photography details to engage the client emotionally and then use the estimate to provide the financial context.

In the sample estimate (Figure 7.2), there are two areas that have increased from the original budget (the telephone handling and response incentives). Be prepared for a reaction from the client and have an explanation from the in-house call centre at hand. Moreover, regarding the response incentives, you can let the client see a sample and show them what the cheaper (and nastier) samples look like.

You should be OK, as the total is below budget. If that is not the case and you venture over the original total, you will need to prepare your justifications and have solutions to reduce the budget (this is very important, as it shows proactivity and consideration for the client's budget).

TIP

You may want to have somebody else inside the organization sign off the client estimate before it goes out – for example, the creative services manager.

Monitoring Costs

Campaigns start and campaigns finish, but they often change their course radically along the way. It is therefore key that you acknowledge this and be prepared:

- The team should be aware of whose job it is to monitor the various cost elements. Normally the account director or project leader is the one who is ultimately responsible for the total campaign budget. It should be clear from the beginning of the campaign that each cost element should be monitored, and if costs look to be going above the budget, warning bells need to be sounded to the project leader.
- If changes are made on the client's side, it is the agency's job to make them aware that there will be cost implications and how high those costs are (either at that stage or, if agreed, later on).
- A record of the client's approval (i.e. signed additional cost estimate) needs to be included in the cost file (this is *essential*).

These three points may appear very simple, but only about 60% of campaigns adhere to them and this is when problems arise. In the heat of a campaign, account handlers do not relish having to bring up the cost issue or cause further delay while additional costs are calculated. This is where it depends on your relationship with your client; how constraining the client organization's financial structures are; and whether you have remained within the original contingency figure.

Whatever the circumstances, you will need to keep the client informed, and honesty, diplomacy and accountability will play important roles.

COMMENT

Remember the previous story of the brochures being sent to Walsall rather than Warsaw? The account director discovered that his executive had phoned through the dispatch instructions to the printers, leaving the message with the receptionist and not following it up in writing.

Not only does the account director have to tell the client about the problem, but she also has to arrange for an overnight air shipment, which costs $2000. Experienced in such matters, she handles it in the best manner possible. Before she rings the client with the bad news, she finds out about the air shipment in terms of timing and costs. The $2000 charge is so that the brochures will arrive in Warsaw in time for the opening of the show. After consulting with a colleague who knows that $2000 is a reasonable price, she gives the go-ahead.

The account director then rings the client to let him know about the situation. The client is a little annoyed, but is reassured that the brochures will be there. In another circumstance (for example, if the mistake had fallen between the agency and the client), the account director would have mentioned the amount that was not going to be charged. This is so the client understood the scale of the problem. However, in this case the amount is not mentioned, as things need to be downplayed.

The next day, the account director convenes a meeting with the printer to discuss what really happened and to see whether the $2000 should be shared with or covered by the printer.

Invoicing the Client

Ideally, invoicing is not done without all the costs having come in and the account team having sent a campaign cost summary/reconciliation to the client. An account team may see this as ideal, but a financial director would not see it as such. It is very much about cash flow. No business will survive without incoming money to counter the outgoings. Every agency needs to avoid being a credit bank for its clients. At the same time, invoices need to be approached sensitively, as they can arrive as potential exploding bombs if they are badly formulated.

Consider the following steps when invoicing. They will help your agency get paid more quickly:

1 Understand what arrangements have been made between you and the client (e.g. look at the contract or talk to your financial director).
2 If there are no existing arrangements, then agree them up front with the client. You will need to make sure that the arrangements are in accordance with the client's accounts department's rules.

TIP

You want to secure cash flow, so you should look to bill certain costs up front:

- All costs that need to be paid in advance before third-party work can commence (e.g. postage, incentives, certain media).
- 50% of the approved estimate, or 50–100% of agency time costs plus third-party costs as they come in.

3 Make sure you have the right address details and the correct name of the person it needs to go to.

4 Make sure that copies are kept and that one set of copies is sent to the client (if necessary). For example, in certain companies the invoices go directly to the accounts department. Therefore you may be delaying payment if you send them directly to your client contact. Accounts departments register invoices and send them to the client. This ensures that the invoices do not sit too long in an in-tray without the accounts department knowing about them.

5 Add any reference or purchase order numbers if requested by the client.

6 Make sure that the client is expecting the invoices (so approval is not delayed through queries).

7 Use diplomacy and sensitivity in formulating the narrative.

8 Ask the following questions:

- Are multiple invoices good or is a consolidated one better (remember the cash-flow implications)?
- Has the client the authority to sign off the total amount of the invoice or only up to a certain amount?
- Is detail good or bad based on your assessment of the client and the campaign?
- Don't forget about the implications of VAT where applicable.
- Are there any campaign elements that will make the client's hackles rise?

9 Agree with the client to hand over (the copies of) the invoices to them at regular face-to-face meetings and take the time to go through them. Make sure that before they leave, any issues are resolved.

10   Agree between the accounts departments and the account team who is going to chase up unpaid invoices, when and with whom.

11   Keep back-ups of all invoice queries.

COMMENT

Remember that, for the agency, the campaign is never finished until all invoices for that campaign have been paid by the client.

TIP

You need to make very good friends with the client contacts who issue purchase orders and process invoices. Make sure you develop a good relationship with them. In the past I have made sure they are on our Christmas card list and have even sent them Easter eggs to thank them for their continued support. I also suggest you develop such a relationship with your accounts department and finance director, as this can reduce the number of internal problems and pressures.

UNDERSTANDING A CAMPAIGN FINANCIAL REPORT

If you are new to account handling, people will refer to what sounds like a 'whip' and you will think you are in for some kinky 'fun and games'. In fact, this is the financial **W**ork **I**n **P**rogress report. This will show you:

- What actual costs have been allocated to a job.
- What purchase orders have been raised to third-party suppliers for future incoming costs.
- What has been invoiced against the costs.
- What has been billed in advance of expected costs.

There are a number of software packages on the market that help you design your own cost/billing spreadsheets. For example, Donovan Data Systems helps agencies report on the financial status of their advertising/marketing campaigns. DDS provides the software for data input and desktop view so that clients and campaigns can be reviewed in terms of financial status (see the example in Figure 7.3).

You will see in the overview report and the detailed cost breakdown the following elements:

- Name of client, product area, job number, relevant dates.
- Agency time vs production costs.
- Agency purchase orders attributed to third-party costs.
- Name of supplier, description of third-party cost, value of cost.
- Purchase orders raised.
- Costs marked up on billing.
- What has been billed and what has been billed in advance.
- Areas of cost.
- Outstanding amounts to be billed.
- Summary total of costs and billing (in the overview report).

If you are smart, you will make sure you are in control of the WIP. Financial control is one of the disciplines of senior management. Make sure you master it at an early stage, as you will be rewarded for it throughout your career in terms of career advancement and uninterrupted sleep. If you don't bother to become an expert in this, you will expose yourself to criticism by senior management (MD and financial director). The finance department should be happy to spend time making you familiar with the principles of managing the WIP. Once mastered, you will realize that it is another political mechanism that you can turn to your advantage.

Bear in mind the following when managing the WIP:

1   Make sure you know who is responsible for issuing purchase orders and authorizing invoices.
2   Don't allow invoices to sit for weeks on end in in-trays.
3   Have regular (weekly?) sight of the campaign WIP report.
4   Meet with the accounts department regularly (weekly?) to discuss the WIP.
5   Match costs against client estimates. Query any overruns with the person authorizing the invoice.
6   Chase up outstanding third-party invoices.

Job Overview

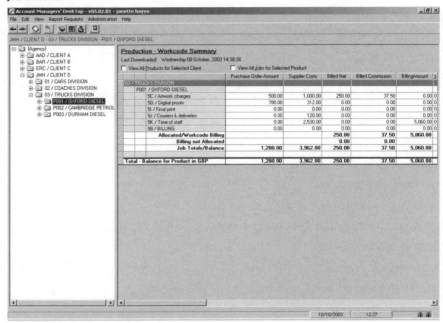

Job Detail

Source: Reproduced by permission of Donovan Data Systems Limited.

Figure 7.3   Dummy campaign work-in-progress report

7   If agency personnel time is monitored by timesheet analysis (i.e. each person working on the job submits a timesheet record to show how many hours each week they have spent on the job), make sure everyone has submitted their time inputs.

8   Be tough with everyone who allows overruns or puts costs on wrong job numbers.

9   Invoice the client as soon as possible (use diplomacy to decide how quickly).

Reconciliation		

We Do Great Work
A G E N C Y

Quarter 1 Campaign Cost Reconciliation
10/3/08

Campaign Element	Budget Cost	Actual Cost
Photography	$10 000	$9 900
Press Ad Production	$13 000	$16 000
Media Space	$750 000	$750 000
Response Incentives	$31 000	$31 000
Inbound Response Handling	$40 000	$35 000
Agency Time (see attached breakdown)	$75 000	$75 000
Legal Approval	$500	$500
Purchase of new freephone number	$5 000	$5 000
Sundries	$5 000	$3 671.67
Contingency	$10 500	–
TOTAL	**$940 000**	**$926 071.67**

* Overrun due to change by sales department of pricing structure. Cost approved 3/02/08.

Figure 7.4   Sample reconciliation

10 Close down or lock the job once it has finished so that no more time costs/extraneous costs can be added.

11 Be aware who is chasing payment of invoices.

12 When writing off costs or closing down jobs with income taken (i.e. allocating an amount to profit), make sure that you have checked the figures thoroughly and have received authorization from the finance department.

Reconciling Campaign Financials

This is a good campaign discipline and also shows the client you are on top of things. It could look something like Figure 7.4 (a simplified version).

UNDERSTANDING AN ACCOUNT'S FINANCIAL METRICS

Each agency will report its financial metrics differently. This section details examples of the key criteria on which an agency will be concentrating to make sure that it is performing well financially:

- Profit and loss (agency-wide).
- Profit and loss (by client).
- Time utilization/billability.
- Work-in-progress analysis.
- Debtors and aged debtors.
- Comparison to previous years.
- Comparison to previous years vs what is forecast.

Agency Profit and Loss

The key indicators for a financial director and outside observers are EBIT and the EBIT percentage (see the sample operating profit and loss statement in Figure 7.5). EBIT is Earnings Before Interest and Tax and is measured against the total operating income. Also of interest is the compensation to income

Operating Profit and Loss

We Do Great Work
A G E N C Y

Operating Profit and Loss for We Do Great Work Agency

INCOME FOR OPERATIONS	
Services billed to clients	
Income from software licences	
Other income	
Total Operating Income	$500 000
COST OF OPERATIONS	
1) Wages/salaries	
Recruitment fees	
Other benefits	
Other personnel expenses	
Total compensation	$300 000
2) Depreciation and amortization	
Facilities	
Other expenses	
Total non-personnel operating costs	$100 000
TOTAL COST OF OPERATIONS	$400 000
OPERATING PROFIT/(LOSS)	$100 000
Management Costs	
(licence to We Do Great Work Agency, New York)	$30 000
EARNINGS BEFORE INTEREST and TAX	$70 000
EBIT% (EBIT/Operating Income)	14%
Compensation: Income%	60%

Figure 7.5   Sample operating profit and loss statement

ratio, which shows what income is being made against what is being paid out for the cost of personnel.

The aim is to increase your EBIT against your operating profit. A percentage to aspire to in the agency world is a minimum of 15%. With the compensation to income percentage ratio, you want to increase your income against your compensation and an agency ambition would be to have a percentage of 50–55%. However, these target percentages really depend on how an agency classifies costs.

Time Utilization/Billability

If an agency has only its people's time to sell, it needs to make sure that its personnel are working on projects that can be billed to the client. Figure 7.6 shows how staff time can be viewed (the staff in this example have been working solely on one client).

Time Utilization/Billability

We Do Great Work A G E N C Y

April 2007 (151.5 hrs)	Total Hours	Non-client	Client	Utilization (35-hr week)	Billability
Account Director	148	38	110	98%	74%
Account Executive	140	91	49	92%	35%
Production Assistant	198	26	172	131%	87%
Copywriter	157	15	142	104%	90%
Art Director	146	14	132	96%	90%
TOTAL	**789**	**184**	**605**	**104%**	**77%**

Figure 7.6   Sample time utilization/billability analysis

This is how utilization and client billability are calculated:

Utilization = total hours worked in time period *divided by* total hours in time period

Client billability = total client hours worked *divided by* total hours worked

The ideal utilization rate is 100%. Bearing in mind training, holidays and downtime, an agency would be happy with upwards of 75%.

In the example in Figure 7.6, you can see from the non-client hours that the account executive has been on holiday and training courses and therefore the production assistant has had to take on extra work in the campaign. Nevertheless, utilization and productivity rates are basically good for this month on the account.

If you then relate the total hours worked to what amount can be billed and the compensation paid to those employees working those hours, you will also be able to create an account's operating profit and loss statement, similar to the agency P/L statement in Figure 7.4.

Work-in-Progress Analysis

WIP analysis is key, as it relates to the fundamental day-to-day survival mechanism – cash flow. This will show whether as costs come in they are being billed immediately on to the client or you are acting as a credit holding bank for your client.

With the client Digital Pipe Cleaner in Figure 7.7, there are two amounts ($1500 and $500) that should have been billed some time ago. This should alert the account team to investigate and get invoicing. It also alerts them to invoice the outstanding $6000.

Client Work-in-Progress Analysis

We Do Great Work
A G E N C Y

Client	Total WIP	Current	30 days +	60 days +	90 days +	Prebilling	Net Effect
Digital Pipe Cleaners	$8000	$6000	$1500	$500	–	–	($8000)
Acme Telecoms Limited	$8000	$6000	$1500	$500	–	$16000	+$8000

Figure 7.7   Client work-in-progress analysis

The account team on client Acme Telecoms Ltd needs to do the same, but they have had the foresight to bill some costs in advance, which puts them in a good situation until they reconcile the job or more costs come in.

Debtor Analysis

You can be very efficient with the WIP and have everything invoiced to the client. Yet if you do not get the client to pay the bills, you will go bankrupt.

In Figure 7.8 there is a big problem with the second client. The agency will need to contact Acme Telecoms Ltd and investigate the problem with payment.

Debtor Analysis						**We Do Great Work** AGENCY

Client	Total Debt	Current Not Overdue	30 days+ Overdue	60 days+ Overdue	90 days+ Overdue
Digital Pipe Cleaners	$20 000	$10 000	$10 000	–	–
Acme Telecoms Limited	$20 000	$5000	–	$5000	$10 000

Figure 7.8   Debtor analysis

Financial Comparison

Normally, reports look at each month individually; the year to date (the total in the months up to the present time from the start of the financial year); and what is forecast (for the month, year to date or to the year end).

BUDGETING AND FORECASTING

When it comes to estimating/forecasting for the year in terms of account income/staffing, it is important that you are comfortable with the figures you submit to the MD or financial director. Ultimately you will be the one responsible for delivering that income with the staff available. You may want to use this step-by-step plan to submit any forecast:

1 Discuss any forthcoming activity with your client (this may follow a planning day between agency and client).
2 Look at the upcoming projects and work out rough budgets (income and production) based on agency and account experience.
3 Decide what personnel resources are needed to execute the forecast activity.
4 Present and discuss your forecast (project costs and staff levels) with your client.
5 After the client meeting, assess the likelihood of the activity happening.
6 Construct a likelihood of income matrix (see Figure 7.9).

Month 3

We Do Great Work
A G E N C Y

Client	Potential Income	100% Likelihood Income	75% Likelihood Income	50% Likelihood Income	25% Likelihood Income
Digital Pipe Cleaners	$47500	$20000	$10000	$15000	$50000

Figure 7.9   One particular month in annual forecast

7 Discuss the income forecast with your boss.
8 Take the financial director through your calculations, letting them understand the activity, staffing levels, issues, uncertainties etc.
9 Keep those involved informed and make sure they are aware of any changes.

EXERCISES

1 Sit down with your finance/account director and ask them to talk through the financial health of the agency/account.
2 Identify three potential improvements to your current financial systems.

STEPPING UP AND OUT

CHAPTER 8

STEPPING UP
AND OUT

In this chapter you will learn about:

- Spotting your next destination.
- Removing the obstacles of hard work and stress.
- Equipping yourself well.
- Moving from managing to leading.

Account handlers at some stage find themselves trying to make the transition from purely implementational skills to directorial expertise. In traditional agencies this has been, for example, the move from senior account manager to account director. You have mastered the craft of running campaigns from start to finish and now you wish to become more strategic on the account. This chapter looks at the transition to a higher position.

Let me give you a couple of examples. George was someone I knew who had shone when he joined the agency as a trainee account executive. He had moved up the ranks and felt he was advancing his career. It was only when he was not promoted after a particular review that he started to question why it had not happened. The questions he asked himself were:

- Is it a corporate 'glass ceiling' I am encountering?
- Am I chasing a job title rather than understanding what the job really entails?
- Am I at the wrong place at the wrong time?
- Am I underperforming?
- Does my boss have something against me?
- Should I leave?

I have also seen the typical high flyer like Susan, who has hardly settled down into a role when she is promoted. We probably ask ourselves in this kind of case:

- Is it luck?
- Is she just brilliant?
- What is she doing that I don't do?
- Does she have a fantastic understanding of networking/politics?
- Why not me?

The answers are really irrelevant, yet no doubt you have asked such questions or are likely to. This chapter helps you create your own luck and gives you sufficient space to move to your desired position.

SPOTTING YOUR NEXT DESTINATION

Some people start in agencies and just keep on going, without really having a plan. If they are lucky, they keep getting promoted and eventually become managing director. More realistically, they may encounter a situation similar to my unfortunate friend George.

I strongly urge you to invest time in developing a personal plan with a mission statement and personal objectives, as discussed in Chapter 6, to try to pre-empt such a conundrum.

TIP

Do you write down your New Year resolutions? If not, is it because it allows you to be flexible? Or is it really because writing down does not commit you to what you have promised yourself? With any of the personal resolutions we are discussing here (mission statement and goals), make sure you write them down. Make sure also that you remind yourself of them so you can monitor your progress. I keep my job descriptions and resolutions at the bottom of my in-tray so when I am regularly clearing it out, I remind myself of what I am there for.

Once you have explored what you are looking for in the next few years (preferably five) in your career, work out how you will achieve it. This is where talking to others will help you gauge the feasibility of your plan.

One forum for discussion about your personal development aspirations is your review. Moreover, there are normally quite a few experienced colleagues on hand to ask advice. Nobody will ridicule you for your ambitions. However 'left of field' the ideas may appear, they will admire you for taking control of your future. I am sure by doing this you could put a few agency heads to shame.

I cannot imagine that all of you reading this will just want to move up to the next level on the same account and in the same agency. Therefore you have to exercise a little discretion when discussing your plans. A series of questions will help to give you the direction for how to pursue your goal:

1   Is the position/destination achievable?
2   In what time frame do you want to achieve it?
3   Are you a credible candidate now (and/or later) for this position?
4   What similarities are there between your current job and what you want to do?
5   What experience/exposure/qualifications will you need to reach your goal?
6   Who can influence your transition?
7   What are the financial implications?
8   How will you know when you have arrived?
9   Are there any shortcuts to your destination (and associated risks)?
10   What is the first step?

I will take an extreme example to emphasize the deliberations you need to go through in planning the route to your next destination.

A friend, Sam, returned from holiday in Bordeaux knowing that he wanted to become a wine merchant in the UK. At that point he was an account manager in a small agency working on a financial services brand. In his mind he believed that becoming a wine merchant was achievable – definitely the first obstacle overcome. Yet Sam realized that he knew nothing about the wine industry and that financial services website experience did not really get him far in his aspirations.

By talking to a wine merchant at a wine-tasting evening, Sam started to understand the business's complexities. Apart from the hurdles of experience, reputation and capital outlay, he still felt his ambition was achievable because he knew he had the right personality traits and enthusiasm for the world of wine.

Sam developed a 10-year career plan to identify his route to becoming a wine merchant. He then detailed the associated economics. For him, this was the acid test of realism as to whether he really wanted to go through with his long-term plan and sacrifice short-term financial gain. He charted the following course:

- Moving to an agency with a wine account to learn everything about the marketplace.
- Getting his great uncle to finance an evening course on viniculture and various trips to European vineyards.
- Setting up his own wine drinker's community website.
- Cultivating contacts in the wine trade.
- Being taken on as an apprentice at a wine merchant's.
- Starting to save his money to amass capital.
- Learning the business of running a wine merchant's for someone else.
- Setting up his own business.

There were hiccups along the way. The agency he moved to lost the wine account within three months so he had to move agencies again. It took some time to get taken on as an apprentice and, though he is not yet running his own show, he has a stake in the wine merchant's he is managing. Every time he encountered any problems, he always referred to what he was trying to achieve and made sure that the solution was a step nearer his goal. At the same time, other people could see his resolve. His great uncle did not come up with the finances for the evening course, but his bank manager did because he could see the plan and Sam's determination.

The reason I use such an example, although it is really tangential to agency careers, is that it shows it is possible to make a large career step if you really want it and you have a good plan. You may say this is too elaborate a process if you want to become an account director from a senior account manager role. You may not have thought about things in the long term if you are focusing solely on the next move. And if you are smart and ambitious, you need to conduct this kind of planning preparation. Don't expect things just to happen, because what does happen may not be to your liking.

If you are experiencing problems like George who wanted to become an account director, I would suggest the following:

- Look at your five-year plan.
- Ask yourself if the account director role fits into your plan.
- Ask yourself if you can achieve and really want to achieve the account director position.
- Ask others if you are a credible candidate for the position now/later.
- Ask your boss for the account director job description.
- Talk to the outgoing/current account director or an account director on another account about the role.
- Identify what the opportunities are within your agency.
- Understand what knowledge/skills/experience you need.
- Identify who can influence your promotion.
- Set yourself a timeframe within which you want to achieve the promotion.
- Discuss your deliberations with your boss.
- Ask for coaching/guidance/training.
- Make sure that all elements express your suitability for that job.
- Check behaviour/attitude/performance.
- Review your communication tone.
- Concentrate on interpersonal relationships (clients, assessors, colleagues).
- Review your language/written work.
- Review your dress code.
- Review regularly whether you are on track for your destination.

REMOVING THE OBSTACLES OF HARD WORK AND STRESS

Frequently people in agencies are working so hard that they don't have time to do the things that are right for their personal career. Some people are working so hard that their personal focus disappears and stress takes over.

If you want to advance your career, you need to create space to step back and see the long term. At the same time, we are in a very hectic and fraught business. Therefore we need to manage our stress levels. In an earlier chapter I talked about becoming more effective through personal organization. Here I will concentrate on reducing unnecessary workload through delegation and controlling work pressures through stress management. Both measures will give you time and space to help advance your career by achieving your goals, as described in the last section and Chapter 6.

Five Myths about Hard Work

1　Hard work never hurt anyone! *Stress accounts for 14% of sickness leave each year.*
2　Hard work is always rewarded. *So why don't agencies pay overtime to account handlers?*
3　People see the hard work. *Not always. Does your boss always know when you come in over the weekend?*
4　Hard work is at least always admired. *Hard work can have negative connotations: 'Why does Sue work so late – is she just slow?'*
5　Hard work will secure client satisfaction. *Maybe working smarter would be more impressive?*

COMMENT

- **Fact 1**: In a recent survey, 29% of workers blamed long working hours for their stress overload.
- **Fact 2**: £5.3 billion worth of productivity is lost each year due to stress.
- **Question**: Is working late paying off for you personally? (Because if so, you are bucking the trend!)

Don't get me wrong. I like hard-working people: they display a commitment and passion that I share and admire. Nevertheless, sometimes people's definitions of hard work to achieve a goal (such as promotion) become 'lots of work' and 'producing stuff' rather than working out what is going to get them to the next level through smart thinking.

I don't want to incite uprisings in agencies up and down the land, but ask yourself these questions:

1   Do you work long hours?
2   Does your client appreciate these long hours?
3   Does your boss really appreciate the long hours?
4   What is your real hourly rate (take-home pay divided by actual hours worked) vs the contractual hourly rate (take-home pay divided by contractual hours)?
5   What is missing from your personal life that you want to stay so late at work?
6   Are these long hours a means to a very rewarding end?
7   Who else on the account works as hard as you do?
8   Do you want to be known as somebody who works long hours?

Let me suggest delegation. If you want to increase your managerial responsibility, you are going to have to use delegation. Even in this time of rationalization and flat structures, you will need to master the art of delegation, even if it is sideways or upwards.

Delegation is a key management skill, so you should be practised in it; in its turn, it will allow you to be more practised in other areas of management. It enables you to concentrate on the things that you want to do or are more qualified to do. And if handled in the right way, it binds your colleagues emotionally into the task and empowers them to think about the project and make future decisions independently (which also frees up your time).

Delegation involves trust and clear communication. Follow these guidelines and they will help you achieve effective delegation:

- **Communicate the specifics of the task**. You would like your account executive to buy a leather whip this afternoon and bring it back to the agency. ('What the . . . ???')

- **Explain the background to the task**. This is for the client/agency fancy dress party. The client has asked if you could procure a lion tamer's whip. ('I understand why now.')
- **Determine the standards**. The executive should pay no more than $10 for it. A mock fancy whip would also do. ('Right, we are not getting into authenticity.')
- **Give authority**. You authorize the executive to get $15 from petty cash, as the client will repay it when he comes in. ('That's the money sorted out.')
- **Provide support**. You suggest that he takes a mobile phone so he can discuss the purchase with you in the shop. ('That's good. I don't want it to be like the Jack and the Beanstalk story.')
- **Get commitment**. You ask him to repeat the request and confirm that he is happy carrying it out ('It sounded bizarre at the beginning, but I get it now and I'll do it my lunch break.')

TIP

Always delegate these things:

- Minor detail work.
- Information gathering.
- Tasks where you are replaceable.
- Tasks that give good experience to others for future responsibilities.

Avoid delegating these things:

- Long-term vision and goals.
- Performance appraisals, job descriptions, coaching.
- Confidential or sensitive situations.
- Assignments specifically allotted to you.
- Confidential or sensitive circumstances.

For more on delegation and moving from managing to leading (discussed later), take a look at *Management for Dummies* (Bob Nelson and Peter Economy, 1996). Although there are many books on the subject, I found this a simple and humorous source for my thinking.

Managing Stress

How many of these phrases do you recognize:

- When I get home, I need a beer or something stronger!
- I don't want to go out, I've had a heavy day.
- I joined the gym but I can never get to it because of work.
- I wake up at the weekend thinking about work.

In isolation these comments could be harmless, but taken in the context of someone who is feeling overwhelmed, they show signs of not coping well and not operating effectively. As I have said before, working in service industries, particularly advertising and marketing agencies, can be very stressful. Some people thrive on what they see as the 'cut and thrust' of a hectic working environment and need the constant pressure of a heavy workload to keep them charged and active. It is when this pressure turns into debilitating stress that problems arise.

Stress could be thought of merely as the modern-day phenomenon of a reduced number of employees with a greater workload, supported and undermined by mobile phones, faxes and e-mails. Yet if we think back to our biology lessons about our caveman ancestors being predators and prey, we can see that biological stress was common in 'fight or flight' situations. We have really not come a long way from those times, with confrontations and threats now arising in the workplace rather than the primeval wilds.

Stress, whether ancient or modern, at home or in the office, is what is experienced when you feel you can't cope with a challenging situation. This situation can be danger, confrontation, change, worries, threats and so on that cause you to believe you are mentally overwhelmed. Interestingly – and this is the significant factor – what is significant is the belief or perception rather than the reality.

COMMENT

How many times have you witnessed somebody 'making a mountain out of a molehill' on account of their emotional state (the broken photocopier, the late delivery etc.)? To them, because stress is the perception rather than reality, the molehill is the mountain. We need to be conscious of this both when we are encountering stress ourselves and when dealing with people who are under stress. Don't exacerbate a potentially explosive situation!

How Stressed Are You?

The key on a personal basis is to identify whether you feel you are continually stressed and to introduce a counter-balance that will allow you to manage your stress levels.

Take Allen Elkin's test in Figure 8.1, using the last two weeks as your time period.

There is a range of literature on the area of stress management in the workplace. If you feel that you are experiencing untenable stress at work or at home, you should take time to solicit advice through books, counselling or colleagues.

TIP

Remember that NABS (the communications industry's trade charity) has an anonymous helpline for those working in advertising who experience personal and professional problems. Simply ring 020 7292 7330.

In the meantime, you may want to think about the following:

- Are you aware that you are stressed?
- Where is the stress coming from?
- Is work affecting your personal life or vice versa?
- Do you understand how your diet could help your physical and mental state?
- Are you getting regular exercise?
- Are you taking regular breaks from work (e.g. lunch away from office)?
- Do you know good relaxation techniques?
- Do you get enough sleep?
- Are you drinking too much coffee?
- Do you limit your alcohol/nicotine intake and not use smoking or drinking as a stress reducer?

Stress Tester

We Do Great Work
A G E N C Y

0 = Never 1 = Sometimes 2 = Often 3 = Very often

Fatigue or tiredness ⬭
Rapid pulse ⬭
Increased perspiration ⬭
Rapid breathing ⬭
Aching neck and shoulders ⬭
Low back pain ⬭
Gritting teeth or clenching jaw ⬭
Skin irritation or rash ⬭
Headaches ⬭
Cold hands ⬭
Tightness in chest ⬭
Nausea ⬭
Diarrhoea or constipation ⬭
Stomach discomfort ⬭
Nail biting ⬭
Twitches or tics ⬭
Difficulty swallowing or dry mouth ⬭
Colds or flu ⬭
Lack of energy ⬭
Over-eating ⬭
Feeling helpless or hopeless ⬭
Excessive drinking ⬭
Excessive smoking ⬭
Excessive spending ⬭
Excessive drug/medicine use ⬭
Feeling upset ⬭
Feeling nervous or anxious ⬭
Increased irritability ⬭
Worrisome thoughts ⬭
Impatience ⬭
Feelings of depression ⬭
Loss of sexual interest ⬭
Feeling angry ⬭
Sleep difficulties ⬭
Forgetfulness ⬭
Racing or intrusive thoughts ⬭
Feeling restless ⬭
Difficulty concentrating ⬭
Periods of crying ⬭
Frequent absences of work ⬭

Your Total Stress Symptom Score ⬭

Your Score

0–19	Lower than average
20–39	Average
40–49	Moderately higher than average
50 and above	Much higher than average

What Could Be Triggering Your Stress At Work

Work overload (too much to do) ⬭
Work underload (too little to do) ⬭
Too much responsibility ⬭
Too little responsibility ⬭
Dissatisfaction with current role or duties ⬭
Poor working environment ⬭
Long hours ⬭
Lack of positive feedback or recognition ⬭
Job insecurity ⬭
Lousy pay ⬭
Excessive travel ⬭
Limited chances of promotion ⬭
Prejudice because of sex, race or religion ⬭
Problems with your boss or management ⬭
Problems with clients ⬭
Problems with coworkers, staff ⬭
Office politics ⬭
A grueling commute ⬭

Figure 8.1   Stress tester

- Are you, colleagues and clients organized enough so you don't create unnecessary workload?
- Do you let people waste your time?
- Have you investigated time management techniques?
- Do you vary your routine?
- Do you have supportive colleagues and friends/family with whom you share problems/issues?
- Do you channel your anger in constructive ways?
- Do you use humour to overcome adversity?

TIP

A recent technique I have developed is when walking to the tube, I think not about all the horrible big tasks that are awaiting me (which I used to do) but what the good things are (however small) and how good I am going to feel about those successes at the end of the day. I find that this stint of positive thinking at the beginning of the day sets me up better than when I used to depress myself before I had even reached work.

COMMENT

The reason I mention that our industry is a stressful one is because it helps to acknowledge this fact and then work out your personal regime to reduce the stress. Take consolation, too, in the fact that that you are not alone. OK, you may have a mental image of stressful stockbrokers sweating under their braces and striped shirts, but don't forget other occupations who have higher stress levels: assembly-line workers, farmers, public service workers, inner-city teachers etc.

EQUIPPING YOURSELF WELL

By following the direction recommended in the last section, you have become the most together, organized and chilled account handler in the agency. So how do you equip yourself to add great value to your colleagues and clients?

You will often hear account handlers and their bosses saying they need more strategic skills. Yet how they get them is not necessarily by simply going on a strategy course. Those coming from business schools or universities have the theory but not necessarily the skills to think, act and recommend strategically. There is no substitute for experience, exposure to good marketing practice and an analytical mind. But how do you get these?

Below are a number of top tips to add to your arsenal of strategic and executional weaponry. What you are trying to achieve is:

- Market knowledge.
- Client knowledge.
- Exceptional knowledge to improve or speed up procedures in the eyes of the client.
- General knowledge/a network to make a more interesting proposition.
- Factors that encourage higher trust in you by your colleagues and clients.

So my tips for developing strategic skills are as follows:

1 Regularly immerse yourself in market information. You should be the CIA agent of the marketing world:
   - Subscribe to and *read* the most important trade press (making sure your reading is up to date before any client meeting).
   - Institute a Wednesday morning Web watch of all major client competitors (and your client's) websites to know what's going on.
   - Attend any free industry or client events.
   - Look out for *Which?* or Mintel-type reports on your client's market.
2 Understand intimately your client's organization, the people involved and the personalities themselves:
   - Get to know your clients personally.
   - Have an up-to-date organogram so you are aware of reporting lines.
   - Read any internal communications magazines.
   - Cultivate a client 'mole'.
   - Understand the real issues and pressures the client is facing.
   - Keep a comprehensive diary and address database for client birthdays, events and meetings (they may be significant for your client but not for you).
3 Understand the dynamics of the advertising and marketing world:
   - Subscribe to and *read* the most important marketing magazines (making sure your reading is up to date before any client meeting).

- Attend marketing events.
- Maintain a contact network of friends in other agencies.
- Scan recruitment ads to understand new accounts for agencies.
- Understand your worth within the marketplace by having regular chats with recruitment consultants.
- Keep interested in other clients' work in the agency.

4 Maintain your general knowledge:
- Subscribe to *The Economist*, *Newsweek* or similar online publications.
- Read the quality daily and/or weekend press.
- Read *Hello!/OK!* magazines or maintain an interest in soaps (you will not be alone).
- Be aware of sporting developments.
- Be aware of the latest DVD/CDs, film releases, books, art shows, plays etc.
- Listen to BBC Radio 4's *Today* programme for a quick summary of up-to-the-minute events.
- Have a news channel as your Internet home page.
- Make a point of doing things you would not normally do to experience a different target audience's viewpoint.

5 Disseminate information:
- Take magazine clippings with you to meetings.
- Circulate e-mails of relevant information (don't get carried away).

6 Cultivate your network and interests:
- Maintain an interest in sport (football is a common currency and a useful passport in many situations).
- Participate in sport. (I wrote off golf 30 years ago when my grandfather said that a lot of business was done on the golf course. How wrong I was! It is stronger than ever. Time to dust off the clubs.)
- Participate in sport or another interest organized by the agency or the client.
- Be part of something that could be of interest to others (e.g. sports club, exclusive dance club, wine-tasting club).

7 Nurture your strengths and work on your weaknesses:
- Be known for specializing in something (e.g. cars, B2B, websites, Swedish dance music).

- Practise your account handling skills away from the spotlight (practise public speaking).

8 Understand other people's mindsets:
   - Spend a day at the client's. Visit retail operations etc.
   - Get involved in a pitch if you have not done one.
   - Understand the dynamics of what the client is looking for.
   - Job swap with people in the agency for a day (ask for this at your review).
   - Put yourself in the shoes of the client's target audience. Use brainstorming and role plays to set the scene.

9 Show star quality.

10 Understand what it takes to influence your profile within the agency and the client.

11 Don't become arrogant.

12 Don't steal other people's glory.

13 Seek to share the glory with clients and colleagues.

14 Align your priorities to your personal goals:
   - Realize that you cannot do everything.
   - Try to work out which 20% of activity will get you 80% of rewards.
   - Understand agency and client goals.

MOVING FROM MANAGING TO LEADING

The last sections have dealt with creating sufficient mental and physical space to help you in the transition from executing campaigns to leading and managing accounts and teams. This is a difficult stage. If we look at the world of football, for example, we see a history of excellent players not making the move to being excellent team managers. Your reputation in the execution of campaigns will help you in becoming a department or team leader. Nevertheless, you have to master different skills to lead. Hopefully along the way you will have been exposed to varying degrees of responsibility, personnel management and financial control to help you understand the difference in roles.

TIP

Take a moment to think about bosses, teachers and managing directors you have seen in action. List their good qualities and their bad traits. What did they achieve? What did they help you achieve? What was their style?

What would be the skills needed to run a campaign versus leading a team?

Implementation skills	Leadership skills
Working well with colleagues	Setting objectives and direction for team
Sense of urgency/timing	Inspiring/motivating
Project management	Supporting/people management
Multi-tasking	Delegation/empowering

Naturally, a number of areas we discussed in the last section about delegation are relevant to leadership, so I will concentrate on other leadership attributes.

Leaders Need Good Analytical Skills

In order to decide on the best course to take, leaders need to be able to work with existing information and also explore new ways to get data.

A colleague uses a technique to make decisions based on defining issues, risks, opportunities, action and responsibility. I have incorporated an example to show how it works.

Issues

The current team's workload is overwhelming. The account director is suggesting hiring an extra person. Otherwise he is going to leave and the client is going to suffer.

Risks

The risks of hiring someone are:

- The work may dry up and not justify additional headcount.
- The client will put business elsewhere.

Opportunities

The opportunities are:

- An extra person will allow the account director to stay and secure new business from client.
- It will allow the team to secure digital experience from the new person.
- It will show that the team boss is listening.

Action

1   Weigh up permanent vs freelance hiring.
2   Talk to finance director about approval.
3   Write recruitment brief.
4   Liaise with recruitment agencies.
5   Interview candidates.

Responsibility

Action 1   Boss.
Action 2   Boss.
Action 3   Account director.
Action 4   Account director.
Action 5   Account director/boss.

NB   The risks and opportunities should be quantified where possible.

Leaders Need Good Communication Skills

Leaders need to communicate the vision or direction for what the team is trying to achieve. If what is being sought is unusual, new or difficult, they need to be clear and inspirational and should produce an easy-to-follow 'roadmap'. This roadmap should have what is expected, when and to what standards.

COMMENT

A good example would be a pitch team leader. Normally pitches happen with little time, with existing client pressures and not having all information at the team's disposal. It is up to the pitch leader to energize the team, get people moving and determine what is expected and when.

Leaders Need to Display Winning Characteristics

They should be optimistic but realistic. They should display confidence. They should show enough integrity, as people's trust is in their hands. They should know how to make decisions. They should also have empathy with the team they work with (i.e. they should understand how they would want to be treated in their situation).

Leaders Need to Empower and Lend Support

A team will function most effectively when each member has a certain scope of individual authority to operate within. Yet leaders also need to know when to give support.

Leaders Need to Manage the Performance of Their Staff

Good leaders need observation and listening skills as regards their team. Staff can then be developed through motivation, evaluation, support and coaching.

15 Ways to Motivate (Agency) People

1   Take a personal interest in the individual.
2   Allow individual ownership of projects.
3   Give valued praise directly to the individual.

4　Encourage clients/colleagues to give praise.

5　Give valued praise in the company of others in the agency.

6　Challenge individuals to greater heights with your personal support.

7　Develop internal awards and/or bonus schemes.

8　Give projects to individuals with a personal interest.

9　Give ad hoc bonuses.

10　Develop team bonding sessions.

11　Take people out to lunch.

12　Take them into your confidence.

13　Acknowledge and respect individual opinions.

14　Expose individuals to the best brains in the agency.

15　Share your vision with individuals and show how they make a difference in achieving that vision.

This last chapter has been less agency specific and I don't apologize for this. I think that leadership is relevant to so many areas of both business and general life that you can grasp the principles whether you are talking about agencies or running a football team. Therefore I would like to summarize this chapter by citing Ernest Shackleton's leadership approach.

Sir Ernest Shackleton is regarded as one of the twentieth century's greatest leaders. For almost two years, he was responsible for the survival of all his men after they were trapped by ice in the Antarctic. He changed his goal from conquering the Antarctic to bringing every single man back alive. At times there were desperate situations, but he never wavered outwardly. He inspired his men to survive, was praised for his individual life-saving decisions, and maintained an integrity that also saw him set off with others in a 22-foot 'glorified' rowing boat on an 800–mile trip to raise a rescue party.

Morrell and Capparell's book on Shackleton (2001) looks at the amazing leadership qualities that helped him turn failure into success (reproduced by permission of Nicholas Brealey Publishing):

The Path to Leadership
... He worked his way into the forefront of a new field. He turned bad experiences into valuable work lessons. He insisted on respectful competition in a business climate that often demanded cooperation.

Hiring an Outstanding Crew

Shackleton built a crew around a core of experienced workers. He conducted unconventional interviews to find unique talent. His second in command was his most important hire. He looked for optimism and cheerfulness in the people he hired. He gave his staff the best compensation and equipment he could afford.

Creating a Spirit of Camaraderie

Shackleton made careful observations before acting. He established order and routine so all workers knew where they stood. He broke down traditional hierarchies. He was fair in his dealings with his staff. He used informal gatherings to build esprit de corps.

Getting the Best from Each Individual

Shackleton led by example. He understood and accepted his crewmen's quirks and weaknesses. He used informal one-on-one talks to build a bond with his men. He was always willing to help others get their work done. He helped each man reach his potential.

Leading Effectively in a Crisis

Shackleton let everyone know that he was in charge and confident of success. He inspired optimism in everyone. He put down dissent by keeping the malcontents close to him. He got everyone to let go of the past and focus on the future. He worked to keep spirits high. He sometimes led by doing nothing.

Forming Teams for Tough Assignments

Shackleton balanced talent and expertise in each team. He ensured all his groups were keeping pace. He remained visible and vigilant. He shored up the weakest links. He got teams to help each other.

Overcoming Obstacles to Reach a Goal

Shackleton took responsibility for getting the whole job done. Even 'Old Cautious' took big risks. He found the inspiration to continue. He kept sight of the big picture. He stepped outside his work to help others.

I strongly urge you to read Shackleton's story. Any obstacle that modern business life can throw at you can be overwhelmed by understanding how Shackleton dealt with those life-threatening elements. He also is a model to study as to how you build a winning team and achieve your goals.

EXERCISES

1 Build yourself a 22-foot boat.

2 Buy some warm clothing.

3 Hire a team you can trust to work with you on delivering success.

EPILOGUE

It is funny how books get written. For instance, I didn't write all of this with the intent of having it published. *Agency Account Handling: Avoiding Blood, Sweat and Tears* came about as a result of consulting between two jobs, when I thought it would be a good idea to put down in writing all the principles and practices I had learned throughout the years as an account handler. I found myself advising on agency/client relationships and could see all the classic mistakes that agencies were making. Moreover, for my next agency I knew I would be going in with the task of helping people become more familiar with such principles and practices. I was also aware I wanted to start breaking out of the mould of traditional client servicing. So I thought it would stand me in good stead to map out the territory of traditional client servicing and then start exploring new paths.

Incidentally, I did not finish off the book before I started the new job. Somebody mentioned that the author Stephen King, in his book on novel writing, suggests leaving what you have written a good while before you read it again. I did this, but it was once again without a specific intention because I suddenly became enveloped in the new job. The literary 'cooling-off' period allowed me to reassess what I had written from the new vantage point of being in a small agency (after a large one) and actually having to 'do client servicing' day in/day out, rather than having the luxury of merely talking or writing about it.

Despite time to change my mind, my view remains the same about what makes great account handling. I think good account handlers know most of the principles associated with effective client servicing. I would be one of the first to say that it is not that complicated; it is really only translating what you expect from any relationship into a business context. What results in great account handling is the personal difference (the calibre of the people involved), plus all those little agency touches that add up to competitive advantage and, essentially, the decision by an individual to concentrate on the right mix of priorities that will produce the right results. In other words, the last ingredient is an account handler's attempt to defy Pareto and deliver 100% by concentrating on the right 20% of personal activity.

I therefore hope that this book helps identify how we can all aspire to great client servicing, whether we find ourselves on new paths or well-beaten tracks.

Good luck!

REFERENCES

Butterfield, Leslie (ed.) (1999) *Excellence in Advertising*, Butterworth-Heinemann, Oxford.

Carter-Scott, Chérie (2000) *If Success Is a Game, These Are the Rules*, Vermilion, London.

Clegg, Brian (2000) *Capturing Customers' Hearts*, Pearson Education, Harlow.

Covey, Stephen R. (1989) *The 7 Habits of Highly Effective People*, Simon & Schuster, New York.

Elkin, Allen (1999) *Stress Management for Dummies*, Wiley Publishing Inc., Indianapolis.

Kaine, J. W. (1998) *Mastering the Art of Advertising Negotiations*, seminar, London.

Morell, Margot & Stephanie Capparell (2001) *Shackleton's Way*, Nicholas Brealey Publishing, London.

Nelson, Bob & Peter Economy (1996) *Management for Dummies*, Wiley Publishing Inc., Indianapolis.

Watling, Brian (2000) *The Appraisal Checklist*, Pearson Education, London.

Wunderman, Lester (1996) *Being Direct*, Random House, New York.

USEFUL INFORMATION SOURCES

The following are trade bodies and organizations associated with raising standards in advertising and marketing. Have a look at their websites for training opportunities as well as for some very useful joint industry guidelines in such areas as research, briefing, pitching and developing legally compliant communications.

The Advertising Association	www.adassoc.org.uk
Advertising Standards Authority	www.asa.org.uk
Association of Publishing Agencies	www.apa.co.uk
British Design & Art Direction	www.dandad.org
British Exhibition Contractors Association	www.beca.org.uk
Broadcast Advertising Clearance Centre	www.bacc.org.uk
The Chartered Institute of Marketing	www.cim.co.uk
Commercial Radio Companies Association	www.crca.co.uk
Committee of Advertising Practice	www.cap.org.uk
The Communication, Advertising and Marketing Education Foundation	www.camfoundation.com
The Communications Agencies Federation	www.cafonline.org.uk
Direct Mail Information Service	www.dmis.co.uk
The Direct Marketing Association	www.dma.org.uk
Incorporated Society of British Advertisers	www.isba.org.uk
Institute of Sales and Marketing Management	www.ismm.co.uk
The Institute of Direct Marketing	www.theidm.com

Institute of Practitioners in Advertising	www.ipa.co.uk
Institute of Public Relations	www.ipr.org.uk
Institute of Sales Promotion	www.isp.org.uk
Internet Advertising Bureau UK	www.iabuk.net
The Market Research Society	www.mrs.org.uk
Marketing Communication Consultants Association	www.mcca.org.uk
The Marketing Society	www.marketing-society.org.uk
NABS	www.nabs.org.uk
Ofcom	www.ofcom.org.uk
Radio Advertising Bureau	www.rab.co.uk
Radio Advertising Clearance Centre	www.racc.co.uk
Royal Mail	www.royalmail.com
Satellite & Cable Broadcasters' Group	www.scbg.org.uk

ABOUT THE AUTHOR

Michael Sims is Client Services Partner at Partners Andrews Aldridge. He has worked both in large and small agencies and has been involved in all areas of account handling, heading up large and small client services departments.

Partners Andrews Aldridge was a relatively new agency when it became the first agency to secure *Campaign* Direct Agency of the Year, the DMA Grand Prix and *Precision Marketing* Agency of the Year at the same time.

Michael was previously at BMP.YCC, The Rapp Collins Partnership, Aspen Direct and Wunderman Cato Johnson. His sector experience covers automotive, telecoms, IT, non-profit and financial services. He has worked on traditional and digital campaigns, consumer and B2B brands, and has led pan-European accounts. Recently he has been associated with ground-breaking work on Lexus and the UK Department of Health's anti-smoking campaign.

Before his agency career, Michael was a teacher and then worked in training and development in the marketing industry. He has also developed training courses for clients to help them work more effectively with agencies of all disciplines.

INDEX